The Circles Story

*How Circles Can Help Your Community Find New
Ways to Resolve Poverty and Thrive*

Scott C. Miller
Founder and CEO of Circles USA

*Stories of personal transformation as told by families,
volunteers, donors, community leaders, staff
members, and researchers*

Contributing Editors

Jan Bodin
Kelly Koepke
Theresa Miller

Proceeds from the sale of The Circles Story will be used for scholarships to help Circle Leaders (those who are moving out of poverty and into economic stability) to attend national and regional Circles conferences.

Circles Annual Conference attended by members from across North America

ISBN-13: 978-1500323417
ISBN-10: 1500323411
1.888.232.9285
www.circlesusa.org

Dedication

This book is dedicated to the 21 authors who contributed their stories in telling *The Circles Story*. A special gratitude also goes out to the Circle Leaders who, confronted with the conditions of poverty, have chosen to pursue a new future and share their insights with their community in order to help others. Thank you for sharing your insights with your community in order to help others find a pathway to economic stability.

Special Acknowledgement

I want to acknowledge my wife, Jan, who has been at my side as the first editor throughout this project. She is a brilliant writer and has served as an ally and confidant since the inception of Circles. Without the love and partnership from her over these past 30 years, I no doubt would have found something easier to do, and would have regretted that decision for the rest of my life.

Table of Contents

Foreword
By Jeannette Pai-Espinosa, President, The National Crittenton Foundation

More than a century ago, Charles Crittenton, a self-made millionaire and social entrepreneur well ahead of his time, dedicated his life and finances to rescue "unfortunate lost girls." He dedicated his energy and finances toward the "betterment of this needy class," which consisted of girls and women being exploited and trafficked for sex, escaping violent relationships, single mothers, homeless girls and immigrant women seeking a better life for themselves. His legacy, The National Crittenton Foundation (TNCF) and the Crittenton family of agencies carries on this necessary work of supporting the needs, and the potential of single women and their children.

In 2013, TNCF marked its 130th anniversary and as we celebrated the work we have done we also recognized that we have not seen a reduction in the tide of women and children needing our support. Data from the Adverse Childhood Experiences survey has proven what we know to be true: there is a direct link between childhood exposure to violence and neglect and adult poverty. This anniversary was a call to action. Fortified with a sharpened focus on health, self-empowerment, economic security and civic engagement, we set out to find a poverty eradication model that would complement and leverage our work. After a lengthy review of various approaches to eradicating poverty, we selected Circles USA.

Why Circles? Let's start with the most obvious reason: It works! Looking at the data of outcomes attained after 18 months of participation in Circles, we can see measurable improvements in people increasing their earned income towards lasting economic security. Moreover, once you spend time talking with Circle Leaders/participants, you understand that the improvement in their lives extends well beyond the balance of their checkbooks. Circle Allies echo the deeply transformative nature of participating in the program in no less meaningful, though different, ways. The outcomes impressed us, but it was the core values and worldview of Circles that really resonated with our experience in supporting marginalized young women and women.

Circles supports families and individuals in pulling themselves out of isolation into a safe community where learning, goal-setting and developing friendly relationships provides the foundation for building better futures for themselves and their families. Participating in Circles provides a powerful opportunity to break down the race, gender, and class barriers that separate us and hold poverty in place. Circles shifts the power dynamic, multiplies social capital exponentially, and changes how we see each other. It's do-able, makes sense, and triggers lasting societal change by addressing the root problems of poverty. The stories in this book reveal the struggle and success achieved by people involved in Circles. The question for you is what can *you* do to be part of Circles once you have finished the book!

Introduction: The Circles Story
By Scott C. Miller

"Can we really resolve poverty?" Is there a DNA code that we need to crack? If so, is it possible that it's already been cracked?

We have enough theoretical and applied research to know how to equip our communities to dismantle poverty. People need long-term support, help with setting and achieving goals, incentives rather than penalties as they leave welfare programs, and a robust job market to earn enough income to be economically stable. The safety net program needs to remain intact while we change the accountability of federal and state programs to moving household incomes to 200% or more of the federal poverty guidelines. The issue is not so much "what do we do?" as it is "how do we develop enough leadership and momentum to apply the sustainable long-term solutions we know will work."

If we continue to invest in an endless series of short-term relief programs without offering solid, long-term programs focused on achieving financial balance, poverty rates will continue to escalate. If we continue funding myriad disconnected nonprofit programs without insisting that they work collaboratively to expand successful strategies, poverty will continue. If our communities use 20th century economic development efforts and educational programs that remain out-of-touch with the emerging economy, more children will grow up to be unqualified for the workforce, thus increasing the burden on their communities. If we remove childcare, housing and food subsidies before people can earn enough income to replace them, we cannot reduce poverty. And if we do not increase the compassion and intelligence of the "haves" regarding what the "have-nots" need in order to fully participate in the economy, then we will continue to pursue misguided and naïve policy and program strategies.

Circles is a way that a local community can bring more people, resources, and influence to solve their local poverty-related problems. In this book, you will hear from a variety of people who have been involved closely with Circles through several different roles and perspectives, including those who are focused on becoming more economically stable (known as Circle Leaders), community volunteers who form partnerships with Circle Leaders (known as Allies), funders, program staff, researchers, and leaders of community organizations.

The federal government's War on Poverty was launched in 1964. Neither the government's programs nor the private sector's economic activity has contributed to reducing poverty. In fact, it is now at record levels. The negative impact of poverty lands directly onto communities. Local leadership must rise up to inform the national dialogue about what is needed to effectively address poverty in our communities. As in all social movements, those who are most affected by the problem must mobilize to provide the urgency and insights necessary to solve it. The impact of poverty is now being felt by millions of middle and upper-income people in so many new ways that the mainstream media is taking notice. Poverty has risen to the top of the public's awareness. It is time to embrace a new and transformative effort in resolving the persistent problems caused by poverty.

We developed Circles to provide a comprehensive, community-driven model that helps people move out of poverty, as well as address the systemic problems that cause poverty. You will learn what Circles is, how it works, how people change when they get involved, and how it can improve your community's approach to poverty.

What happens if you don't personally get involved?

Research shows that poverty is the single greatest threat to children's wellbeing. Although we want to have faith that the government and social services are tackling the underlying causes of poverty, the reality is that we have more than 16 million children grow up below federal poverty guidelines, which are currently set at $23,550 a year for a family of four. Research also shows us, however, that the average family needs twice this amount to meet their basic needs for food, housing, healthcare, transportation, utilities, and clothing. Given that standard, 45% of all U.S. children are being raised in low-income homes with parents who are working but unable to meet basic needs consistently. In other words, half of the country is in financial jeopardy. For a nation built on the principles of capitalism and entrepreneurial ingenuity, it is ironic how many people go through our educational system without learning the fundamentals of capitalism or entrepreneurialism. It's like being asked to live in the ocean without swimming lessons.

Unfortunately, our public schools systems have not been able to provide an effective combination of educational and enrichment programs to our impoverished communities. In addition, children raised in poverty have higher levels of physical and mental health issues. We should not be surprised that as teens and young adults they are less able than their middle and upper-income peers to find and keep well-paying jobs.

When we allow such a large number of children to be raised in poverty, our community's economy is negatively affected. For example, the Baby Boomers have been a huge economic force, able to generate good incomes in their communities from an abundance of white and blue-collar jobs. According to the Pew Research Center, 10,000 Baby Boomers turn 65 every day, and will continue to do so through 2029. Because they only had 1.7 children per household, a new demographic crisis in America has begun to unfold that directly affects our economy as there are fewer trained workers to take their place. In short, there will be more good jobs than people who have the qualifications to fill them.

The well-paying blue-collar jobs have diminished, too, leaving low-paying service jobs in their wake. Well-paying jobs now require higher qualifications, primarily academic degrees in science, technology, engineering, and math. Children being raised in poverty typically do not perform in school as well as their middle and upper-income peers. With fewer qualified people available to generate income in communities, and more unqualified people requiring subsidies, many communities are facing a major economic crisis. When there are more people functioning as dependents than there are those working and paying taxes, there is simply not enough money to provide basic municipal services like repairing streets, and funding schools, police and fire departments. Property values will diminish as businesses are unable to expand, and new businesses are harder to attract. More people with wealth will leave the community and many who are in poverty will stay.

For the first time in recent U.S. history, solving poverty is no longer just a humanitarian effort. Solving poverty is an economic imperative that our communities must embrace in order to keep going.

Ellie Reiter, the youngest attendee at the most recent Circles Annual Conference, prepares to get mobilized as she reads over the schedule. Can we end poverty in her lifetime?

Chapter 1: Telling our Stories

"Scott, you have to tell people right away in your presentations why you are working on solving poverty problems. You don't look, sound, or come off like someone who ever experienced poverty, so people need to know why you have committed your life's work to doing something about it." This came from a colleague at an Asset-Based Community Development workshop led by John McKnight and his colleagues. She was right, and my story does need to be told before I lay out any ideas on what we can and should do about poverty.

I grew up in the suburbs, free of concerns that our family would not have enough money to pay the bills. Both my parents had professional jobs and they were very good financial managers. I never worried about money. I have, however, experienced the emotional poverty that afflicts millions of others from the suburbs who, at times, have placed work above relationships as they incessantly chase the American Dream. So often, this pursuit can lead to an empty despair if it is done at the expense of fulfilling a deep sense of meaning and a strong sense of community. That was my challenge, which led me into this incredible journey with Circles.

Stories are what transform the world. Our brains light up like fireworks when we are listening to a story. So let me begin with mine, followed by many others who will give you a strong introduction to Circles and how it can help your community address poverty in a new and powerful way.

A View from the Suburbs
By Scott C. Miller

Why is this white guy from the suburbs talking about ending poverty? It initially does not make sense to most people. And given that I never knew poverty personally, it is a legitimate question. Like many millions of Baby Boomers who were raised with the social advantages of being white, male, middle-class, and well educated, I never gave one thought while growing up to the problems of poverty. I had some vague explanation in the back of my belief system that said people get whatever they deserve. Who knew that events in my life would cause me to dismantle my naïve notions about the causes of poverty and lead me into the wonderful world of Circles?

At age 11, I could not believe how exciting it was to open my first cassette tape recorder! I had sold 70 boxes of all-occasion cards up and down the streets of our suburban neighborhood and this amazing piece of equipment was the reward for my efforts. I loved everything about it, the way it looked, the ability to record songs right off the radio, and I could even make my own soundtrack for our haunted houses. It did not get any better. I was hooked on setting sales goals and achieving them. I sold enough boxes of cards in the following year to get a microscope kit, chemistry kit, a gas-powered small racing car model, and an archery set. The message was loud and clear: *motivation and hard work will get you what you want in life.*

My siblings and I belonged to scouting groups, music bands, and sports teams of all kinds. All of these activities required fundraising events and we learned to sell Christmas trees, jellybeans, boxes of oranges and grapefruits, and even gold-painted hangers. We were exposed to an ever-growing network of kids and other adults who reinforced the value of goal setting. We had to adapt and compete in order to make our way through an abundance of opportunities that life in the 'burbs afforded us. We never questioned that we deserved everything that came to us or that there was any limit to what we could accomplish. *Work hard and get whatever you want.*

The Miller kids, 1966 (Warren, Teri, Scott, and Hal)

Being raised in an upper middle-class home by two professionals with college degrees creates an air of confidence about finances. I never questioned that I was going to college and would make at least as much money as my suburban peers. My parents were raised during the Depression and post-Depression years, so they had amazing savings skills. They raised all four of us on my dad's salary and banked my mom's so they could send us all to college. By the time I graduated from high school in the mid-seventies, I had personally saved $2,500 for college. My parents used their savings to cover tuition, books, room, and board. My money was used for critical out-of-pocket expenses, like a new stereo, pizza, and beer.

I didn't know what I wanted to do, but I had artistic ability and was good in math so it was suggested that I consider architecture. I enrolled in the Honors College and the Architecture Program at Kent State University. Both of my parents were from Northeast Ohio and had graduated from KSU. It was a familiar part of the country to me and I had a lot of extended family in the area. School had never been that difficult for me so I was accustomed to getting good grades without much struggle. The course load that I took on in college, however, was a different story. Honors classes were difficult enough, but the architectural courses were especially challenging

3

for me. For the first time, I was over my head and the pressure was taking its toll on my emotional health. By the end of the first year, I felt depressed and sought counseling.

The counseling I went through was by far the most powerful "course" that I took at KSU. I had the good fortune to work with someone who taught me how to do what I wanted to do rather than what I thought I should do in life. He emphasized the value of taking more time to have fun in order to balance my very strong work ethic. He questioned whether I was happy or not with my life choices. He encouraged me to focus on my relationships and to slow down enough to enjoy my life.

During Christmas break of my second year of college, I fell back into a depressive cycle and a friend suggested that I focus my attention on helping others. He recommended volunteering at the Catholic Worker in downtown Rochester, New York, which was 11 miles from my hometown of Fairport. I had no idea that this first encounter with people living in destitution would have such an influence on the direction of my life's work.

I left the architectural program and moved into the Organizational Behavior program in the Business College, which better suited my interests. After graduation, I secured jobs in the nonprofit sector and eventually took a position to provide counseling and financial assistance to people in immediate crisis. The volunteer work I had done at the Catholic Worker gave me enough experience, context, and insight to help me land the job. Because of my own recent personal journey, I had a high level of compassion for people I was meeting. Having successfully moved through my own feelings of despair, I also possessed a strong confidence that people could overcome anything, or so I thought.

By the time I completed my first 50 interviews, I had distributed all of the financial assistance money budgeted for the month in just 10 days. I was emotionally exhausted by the stories that I was hearing. People had let me into their worlds and most of them had struggled with more pain than I had ever known. Poverty had been devastating for them and their families and they had become stuck in the "tyranny of the moment."

What made matters worse was that there were no solutions in the community to help them get out of poverty. All of the programs, including the one that I was now running, were designed to help people temporarily manage poverty. Job training programs did not help many people actually get good jobs. Much of the community thought like I used to think: if you work hard, you get whatever you want and need. Human service programs had been shaped by middle-class people who shared this worldview and offered pseudo-solutions for people who were experiencing poverty.

The vast majority of the people who came to our agency for help had been raised in poverty. They did not grow up in the white, stable neighborhoods in the suburbs with all of the financial advantages that I had enjoyed. If life were a baseball game, it was fair to say that I was born on third base and led to believe that I had hit a triple to get there. My clients were born out in the parking lot and many didn't even know how to get into the game.

I knew then that we had to organize the community in a new way so that we could help people solve the underlying problems that were keeping them trapped in poverty. I attended a presentation by a community action agency about their struggles to help families out of poverty. They had asked many of their clients if they had gotten out of poverty and were discouraged to learn that only a small number had. Many of them had married someone with a job. Should the agency abandon their 50-plus different programs and start a dating service?

The agency decided to go to people's home with caseworkers that they called Family Development Specialists, and build a relationship that would be strong enough and last long enough to make a difference. This relational strategy made great intuitive sense to me and I began to promote it in Ohio. Within a couple of years, we had raised over a million dollars to pilot the Family Development model in five major urban centers within the state.

We were able to show that people were getting jobs, going back to school, or at least getting counseling so that they could go back to school and get better jobs. We were focused on the right outcomes and getting good results. Unfortunately, most of the foundations funding the effort were only interested in a three-year investment cycle, which did not give us enough time to build sustainable funding from mainstream sources.

My colleagues in Iowa invited me to join them. They had just secured a new federal grant and had piqued the investment interest of the Annie E. Casey Foundation. By January of 1992, my wife, Jan, and I were settled in the middle of Iowa and I was learning how to apply my organizational development degree to consulting with anti-poverty agencies. We started a program called Move the Mountain with major funding from the Casey Foundation.

Organizers hope to move a mountain

"We realize that only together can we move a mountain, and only together will we be able to transform this system so that it's far more effective."
— *Scott Miller, director of Move the Mountain*

Story headline in local Iowa newspaper, 1992

Our hypothesis was that while there was plenty of money and talent available to the system that addresses poverty, the goals and approaches were fragmented and the results were lackluster. By working with the leadership of the system, we thought that we could get strategic plans to overlap and form powerful collaborations that could attract new resources, generate innovation, and reduce poverty in the region. After a year of pursuing strategic plans, we noticed how difficult it was for the schools, human service agencies, and government programs to engage the community in planning. There was very little effort to involve people in poverty in meaningful dialogue. We decided to tackle these problems with the partnership of over 30 low-income participants involved in regular planning sessions with us.

By 1995, we started a program designed to help people off welfare. We were having good success in attracting people to weekly mutual support meetings, but they were not getting off welfare. To help, we brought in mentors. In some cases, the mentors made a positive difference, but many of them were out of their element and overwhelmed by the circumstances of the families that they were assigned to help. They needed better training and we needed a different approach to channel the goodwill of volunteers without causing additional problems for everyone.

"Why don't you take a look at Circles of Support in Canada?" asked one of our consultants, Mike Green from Asset Based Community Development. He thought that what they had done to support people with disabilities to live more independently and avoid being placed in institutions might fit nicely with what we were doing. There was something wonderful about this idea. I remember thinking that this might be how communities could actually reduce poverty.

All of us use the process of building circles of relationships in our lives. Often our social circles provide information and contacts that help us find better jobs, housing, and other opportunities. It is a natural instinct in human beings to create a sense of belonging through our connection to family and social groups. Our friends and family reinforce our worldview. We tend to mingle with people who are peers and agree with our strong values and assumptions about how the world works. We tend to join or form groups with people who have similar income levels. It is rare to have a strong friendship with people who have much or less money than we do. The intent of Circles is to normalize these otherwise awkward relationships because we know that they can make the most difference in reducing poverty in our community.

We invited the participants of our weekly meetings to develop a Circle to have two to three volunteers supporting them. We began to train volunteers to become Allies rather than mentors. The emphasis was not on fixing a family but rather on listening, supporting, showing interest and then asking what they could do to help, rather than jumping in and prescribing change.

Circles was soon making a difference and getting noticed for its results. We were asked to spread the Circles approach throughout the network of Community Action Programs. We had to learn how to talk about not only what we did, but what steps we took to start Circles. It was not easy for organizations that had decades of expertise in managing federal grants and delivering emergency relief services to find their way back to the roots of community action. For groups that did not have ready partnerships with local employers, the task of helping people out of poverty through better jobs was both new and difficult.

Circles required an organizational ability to find innovative funding that would support solutions rather than short-term band-aids. It also demanded that groups mobilize and support volunteers, move people into viable job and career paths, and facilitate the changes that people would have to go through in order to move from the crisis-orientation of poverty to the goal-centric road to economic stability. Several of the early new Circles programs came and went without being sustained. We became more selective in the kinds of organizations and conditions required before we could help communities build an intervention like Circles. And we learned what others needed from us in order to build a solid foundation.

One morning while I was having coffee with a Circles' staff team in Sandpoint, Idaho, someone commented that they thought the word "participant" was demeaning and that there had to be a new title for the role. After a few minutes, the title "Leader" emerged in our discussion. Since we wanted people to lead their own Circles rather than passively accepting direction from Allies, the new term would reinforce the actual nature of the relationships for all involved. We were also asking people to provide leadership in the community by telling their story to decision-makers in hopes of changing the fragmented nature of the services in the anti-poverty world.

To want to help others who are helping themselves is a natural impulse in most human beings. However, the impulse can become manipulative and unhelpful when we expect people to change using only the ideas that we think are best to use. The evolution of any relationship can move from an initial euphoria to some disappointments as we get to know each other better. If we decide to stay in the relationship, we often find that our expectations of each other become more realistic and we can see more clearly how to have a productive experience. We invited people to give themselves at least six mistakes a day, creating a culture of learning rather than struggling with any false hopes of "getting it right" all the time.

By 2008, Circles was being implemented in 40 communities across the U.S. and parts of Canada. Numerous organizations were building it into their existing budgets, while others sought new research and development funds. By 2013, the number of communities embracing Circles had doubled and Move the Mountain's name was changed to Circles USA.

Thousands of people have invested their time, resources, and talents into co-designing Circles with us so that people have the support that they need to transform their lives. Once we are in relationship with people who have been raised in a different world than ours, we can never see our world the same again. I firmly believe that we can end the conditions of poverty in the U.S. and, eventually, abroad. As North Americans, we have a unique opportunity and obligation to address our poverty with effective solutions rather than placing one band-aid after another on a serious wound.

May the stories that follow inspire you to stop thinking that there is nothing that can be done to eradicate poverty. Instead, know that you are in a position to make a significant difference, if you take action in your community.

Join or start a Circle!

Darion gives the "field goal" sign at a Circles evening program in New Mexico

Chapter 2: What Is Circles?

There are five basic steps to Circles:

1. **Enough!** We know that 40% of our success is based on Circle Leaders' readiness to change. But Circles is also interested in the readiness of the community to change so that it stops generating so much poverty. We look for community members who have "means" to step up and do something because they have had enough of the lousy outcomes that poverty has brought so many people in their community.

2. **Pick Your Number.** We encourage everyone to pick a monthly income number that will cover all their basic expenses and save for the future. This number is usually at least 200% of the federal poverty guidelines. For a single person, this would be $1,975 a month, or $11.67 an hour. For a family of four, this would be at least $3,975 a month, or $23.85 an hour. The plan that generates $11.67 or $23.85 an hour is drastically different than the plan that generates minimum wage.

3. **Expand Your Circle.** We provide people with weekly meetings that offer a meal, childcare, and a support group of both peers and community volunteers who are Allies in helping people achieve their financial goals. The magic of Circles is the community building that develops and sustains relationships long enough to transform people's lives.

4. **Work Your Plan.** What will it take to become economically stable? Circles encourages people to develop a written plan that moves them towards better jobs and more income. We also help people become financially literate, manage their increased income more effectively, and build assets. People are asked to participate for at least 18 months in order to

achieve their long-term goals. Circles is available as a support system for as long as people want and need it.

5.   **Be an Ally.** Everyone is encouraged to pay it forward by supporting others. Circle Leaders are given opportunities and supported to lead in community events, planning, and service on organizational boards in order to bring their insight and urgency to solving poverty.

Circles Leaders go through a 12-week class to prepare an individualized economic stability plan. People begin by reconnecting to their dreams for their family's future. Through SMART (specific, measurable, achievable, relevant, and time-bound) goal setting and budgeting work, they begin to outline their plans to bring these dreams into reality.

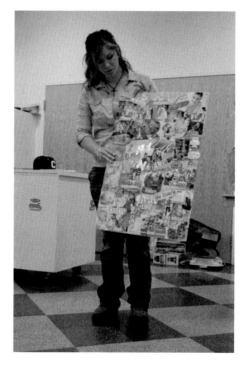

Sarah showing her Future Story Plan at a Circles meeting in Davidson County, NC.

Community volunteers are trained as Allies who support Circle Leaders to achieve their goals in a non-paternalistic manner. Circle Leaders lead their Circle by convening regular meetings and asking Allies for what they need to help achieve their goals.

The Big View is a monthly meeting focused on educating the community about barriers such as the *financial cliffs* that occur when people leave welfare and other subsidy programs. Policy makers are educated to the benefits of providing a pro-rated exit plan for all subsidy programs in order to allow people to afford paying for new health insurance, childcare, etc. with their new earned income.

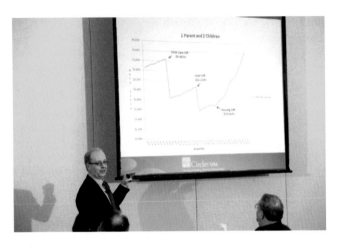

Scott presenting to an audience in Michigan the trauma of financial cliff effects as people make their way off subsidy programs.

Through the Circles community, people learn about new community resources that can help them to achieve their goals. Circles doesn't duplicate anything that is already in the community. Instead, we broker these resources so that people can put them into their long-term plans. Community programs use Circles as a "warm hand-off" so that their services can be woven into the long-term plan.

So, What Do They Actually Do In Circles?
By Katie Woods and Ginny Giles of Good Samaritan Ministries, Circles Ottawa (Michigan)

In Circles, individuals with low incomes who are motivated to become economically stable are called Circle Leaders. Tim found Circles through an organization that serves formerly incarcerated men and women. Tim has been working hard to better his life, and he's succeeding.

Jay and Tim

Tim is paired up with Jay, his Circle Ally. Jay is a neighbor who joined Circles to offer encouragement and support to Circle Leaders as they achieve their financial goals. This partnership has given Tim the strong relationships and confidence he needs to take classes at Michigan Works and spend time with a local electrician – what Tim hopes to become. But it's not all about him. Tim is in Holland's Neighborhood Leadership Academy in Michigan, learning how he can lead efforts to build a stronger community. Most importantly, Tim cares about being a good father to his children. Tim has hopes for his life that he never dreamed of several years ago.

How does all this wonderful work happen?

At around 6 p.m. on Thursday evenings, Tim meets up with Jay, his Ally and neighbor, at Moran Park Church. When Circles came to town, he saw it as an opportunity to keep the momentum going on his path to recovery and a better life.

From 6 to 6:30 p.m., everyone eats dinner together. "I enjoy the people there. We're like a family." Tim says of the group. Everyone needs a family.

At 6:30, everyone wraps up their dinner and gathers in a circle to convene the meeting. Each person takes a turn to tell the group about something new or good in their life.

When that's finished, the group begins that night's special activity. Sometimes they have a guest from Fifth Third Bank help them learn a skill that could help with their financial goals, like using a savings account. Other times they discuss those things that are bigger than their individual situations – like laws and policies – which affect their ability to escape poverty. But most of the time, the Circle Leaders take time with their Allies to combine their efforts and further the Leaders' specific goals and aspirations. Tim has set big goals for himself and his time with Circles. What he really wants to do is be an electrician and own his own business, but he isn't really sure how to make it happen. "I benefit from [Jay's] tutelage. He knows some of the little details about starting a business that I don't and he holds me accountable," Tim says of his relationship with his Ally, Jay.

Jay agrees. "More importantly, we encourage each other. We share life and our spiritual journeys. Each time we meet we check in on the progress of our respective plans," Jay says very seriously. "My life is better because Tim is in it."

Then comes Tim's favorite part of the night, the appreciations. The group gathers in a circle again. This time it's to offer mutual encouragement and support to everyone in the group. It's important to the group to end the night with words of affirmation that empower the Leaders to go out and take the steps necessary to accomplish their goals.

"When we create a culture of 'together we can' thinking, we can achieve almost anything," Ally Jay says of Circles. "We have each other's backs and together our gifts will matter to each other and our neighborhood."

Luncheon event in Holland, MI where Scott Miller invited the community to help at least 10% of their children out of poverty, potentially causing a tipping point in the eventual eradication of their poverty.
(They accepted the challenge.)

Chapter 3: The Stories of Circle Leaders

Based on our Circles research, we know that people must have myriad supports in order to leave poverty for good. Circles provides weekly meetings, peer support, allies, networking, job preparation, placement, and post-placement coaching, as well as the opportunity to build leadership skills that can be used in all aspects of life. We teach and reinforce sound financial management and long-term goal setting.

From Poverty To Prosperity
By Rebecca Lewis, Circles McPherson (Kansas)

Rebecca Lewis has made the journey from being a single mom in poverty to becoming a local Circles Coach and a member for Circles USA Board of Directors. Her insights have influenced the dialogue among board members, our national training team, and colleagues across our network. Rebecca's story, as told from the view of someone who was able to use Circles to get completely out of poverty, is both inspiring and informative as to what is required if we are to eradicate poverty.

I have wrestled with poverty since birth. When I was 16, I decided to quit school and move far away from both my family and a predominantly middle-class town to seek my "house on the hill." Much to my surprise and dismay, instead of finding a new career and home, I found an abusive marriage and a hardcore drug habit. After 13 damaging years, I left my husband with only the clothes on my back. Not long after, I found myself pregnant with my first child.

Bound and determined to create a brighter future for my newborn child, at age 29 I enrolled full time in college. Unfortunately, as a single mother of an infant, working full time and going to school, I continued to suffer from a life of too few resources and the demand it requires. The daily challenges of single parenting, and the resentment I felt at being powerless to stop the poverty cycle, fueled my daily fire to persevere.

Rebecca Lewis and her children

In the summer of 2010, I received a letter from my school that I had maxed out my financial aid and if I wanted to finish my bachelor's degree, I would have to pay tuition for the two remaining semesters. Up until then, I had been instructing art in the summer and working as a janitor at the college. I was devastated, but determined. I picked up a job tending bar and set up a payment plan with the university. Around the same time, I stopped by a church that I frequented, for diapers for my youngest.

I had built a relationship with a very kind secretary there, and on that day I began to share with her how much getting those diapers meant to me and how someday I was going to finish school and claim a better life for my children. Once I did, I vowed I would come and give back. She lovingly pointed to a flyer that said something about a class to get out of poverty.

My first thought was, "What are these people going to teach me about poverty that I don't already know!" My second thought was, "Man, I've gotten so many diapers from this lady I better sign up!" So I did. Deep down I was convinced that once I took my seat in the class, I would show the instructors I was already doing everything in my power to get out of poverty.

I quickly realized this was true…I was doing everything *I knew* to get out of poverty. I also realized that I was an expert survivalist. To my shock, it became apparent that I really knew very little about any other economic class than my own. The concept of sustainability was as familiar to me as an African roadmap and I certainly could not tag the word *thriving* to any compartment of my life, save my spirituality. I also found I was a master at putting out fires, but very inept as to how to keep them from igniting in the first place.

I entered the Circles fellowship scared, broken, overwhelmed, exhausted and very suspicious of the "middle-class" leadership and presence. I left the first night with a boost of hope I had never before experienced in my struggle to end poverty. I also felt a strong connection to others and was able to honestly admit how alone and vulnerable I had been.

Every day, until Circles, I felt as if someone was erecting a sky rise on my shoulders, and that soon something was going to give. My three boys, ages nine, five and two, and I lived in an antique trailer, which sported holes in the floor, broken windows, a faulty water heater and had heating and cooling bills you would expect from a 5,000 square foot home. The car I owned was faithful to nothing but breakdowns. I was gone at work or school five to six nights a week, which meant dragging children home late in the evening from the babysitter. My school-aged children struggled with behavior, and later the oldest and the youngest were diagnosed with autism. Motherhood, for me, felt like a failure, and every moment seemed held together by threads. The only dream that I could find energy to muster was when I might be able to take my next nap.

By the time I graduated phase one of Circles, against my initial hesitance, I fell in love with the organization, my classmates and yes, even the "middle-class" people who made it all happen. On graduation night from Circle Leader training, my emotions and love for the organization swung my pendulum in a complete opposite direction than I had planned, so I signed on for 18 more months of Thursday nights and the uncomfortable idea of "Allies" in my life. Two years later, the woman who filled that Ally role, I now call a dear friend.

I am personally convinced that one of the biggest forces driving this non faith-based program is prayer. During the course of Circle

Leader training, my boss walked up and handed me two raises, for no reason, totaling a $5 an hour increase. The second time it happened, I thought to myself, man, those people at Circles must be praying for me! I had been on a HUD waiting list for a housing voucher for over two years and suddenly it became active and the boys and I left the trailer park for a safer, nicer four-bedroom home. Also, a very kind soul helped me get a safe and dependable car. After all of this, we were driving to Circles one night and my oldest son piped up from the backseat, "Why are we going to Circles tonight, mom? We're not poor anymore!"

In 2012, I walked the stage at my college graduation – the first person in my family, immediate or extended, to ever obtain a four-year degree. A few months later, a job became open for the Circles Coach. Suddenly, God's plans for my whole life became clearer. I was standing at a Circles gathering one night and someone was telling me how they felt God led me to the job, and for a moment it was like room stood still. I replied, "Ya know, it is like everything I have gone through in my life makes perfect sense now." I had found my calling and now I work daily with others who have similar stories to my own. They draw from me and I am emotionally filled by being of service to them.

Late December of the same year, the pastor of the church that housed our Circles office called me and asked me if I would accept the position as the Outreach Coordinator to run the diaper and food ministry. The first time I went to Wal-Mart and filled up the cart with diapers, I could not stop the tears from streaming down my face. Now, I am the kind lady who helps moms and babies with diapers when they come to the church. And yes, I tell them about Circles.

A month later, my oldest son had a psychotic breakdown and I found myself driving my 10-year-old little boy four hours away to stay at a children's mental hospital. I worked late at the bar that same evening, and when I got off and went home, tears welled up in my eyes as I faced the front porch. I felt so empty and I dreaded going in the house. When I got to the front door, there was a package there. It was from my Ally. I picked up the pretty bag, and suddenly did not feel alone opening that door. I know God had sent her just when I needed her. I am grateful.

I also set long-term goals with my Ally. I was to access dental treatment and complete the necessary appointments to get my teeth healthy. Thirteen appointments and $1,700 later, I reached that goal. Another goal I set was to get my children and myself out of poverty. The third goal I set was to buy a home. I added up all the times I have moved in my life, and from what I can remember, the number is 71, not counting the times I lived in my car. I was 38 years old when I tallied the moves. My oldest son, who was nine at the time, had already moved 11 times.

In January 2014, Circles of McPherson County was able to hire me full time. I was still working three jobs, but my sons and I had officially left generational and economic poverty. While I have not yet been able to buy a home, I know that in time, it too will happen. Currently we have been in the same house for over two years. That is a record and we feel stable.

I am beyond humbled to sit here and pound out on my keyboard the highlights of my story. I am even more honored to be a part of all of my Circles' families' transformations. The other day I heard a plug on the radio about a "dream job." I had to stop and call my Director and tell her I was living my dream job. She agreed. She was, too! She is a big part of the reason for my love to come to work every day. I am part of a movement in our community to solve poverty for its members. Most of the Circle Leaders in our program have become my friends.

Shortly after I accepted the position as the Circles Coach, I convinced my mother, at age 58, to sign up. She had misgivings to say the least, and of course she verbalized how getting out of poverty at her age would be impossible. What her participation meant was that at every Circles gathering there were three generations from my family under one roof working our way out of poverty.

My mother was five years old when she was thrust into poverty by a divorce. She, too, has struggled almost every day of her life to just survive and she has also been plagued with chronic health issues since childhood. A few years ago, my dad's health took a sharp turn and he was placed in a nursing home. My mother was left to manage the broken pieces. I am grateful that during this unrelenting transition, she had the Circles community to spur her forward.

Now here is the most remarkable part of my Circles journey yet. My mother, who already has one part-time job, began another part-time job yesterday. Once she gets her first paycheck, all on her own, she will cross the poverty threshold to middle class. Not one time in their entire marriage have my parents ever been completely out of poverty! I cannot describe how amazing this feels. In the checkout line at the store, or driving down the road, a little voice in my head says, "Rebecca, you're not poor anymore, nobody in your family is poor anymore!" It's almost unbelievable. The other night I was sitting with my oldest watching a cartoon and one character said to the other, "You poor insolent child." The other character fired back, "I'm not poor! We're middle class!" My kid turned to me and said, "Mom! That's like us! We're middle class!" Bottom line, the children know we have worked our way out of poverty as well.

I have learned so much over the past two and a half years. I have learned that first and foremost, that I, and many others who are fighting to survive, need a group of people to surround us and lift us up. I have learned that each individual, once placed in that circle, begins to thrive and bloom. I have learned that poverty is not just the individual's problem experiencing it. It is the community's and nation's problem as well. I am also convinced that if you build a circle of support around someone who wants to get out of poverty, they can and will. And if you teach people who are not living in poverty what poverty truly is and is not, they will begin to take ownership and work to solve it.

America, you need me to tell you there is hope for the direction our nation is going. You need to hear that there is still an American dream and that families on the lowest rung of the economic ladder can still lasso that dream. A couple of years ago, I would have grimaced at a conversation like that. Today with tears in my eyes, I can tell you I am living proof.

Nursing a Young Woman's Dream – To Be A Nurse
By Susan Garrett and Mark Robertson, ABCCM *Our Circle*, (Buncombe County, North Carolina)

Many different kinds of organizations bring Circles into their programming in order to provide people with a more holistic and long-term support system. Circles is not a faith-based program, but rather it encourages a diverse community-building process that welcomes all people from the community to join. Yet, faith-based organizations do use Circles to "walk their talk" and to give their members an opportunity to serve others. Here is an example of a faith-based organization in North Carolina using Circles.

When you experience Danika's bright eyes, ready smile and positive attitude, you would never imagine the trials she has come through and all the ways she has persevered. Danika was in school at North Carolina Agricultural and Technical State University but then lost her focus on schoolwork and had to withdraw. To make matters worse, when she dropped out of college, she became homeless as well. This led to a period of couch surfing at friends' houses, all because her pride would not let her disappoint her mother and come back to her home in Asheville. She got a job working at a McDonald's first and third shifts so that she could sleep in between when her friends weren't home.

After six months, she applied for her first apartment and was striving to be self-sufficient, but then she got pregnant. Suddenly, Danika was about to be a single, homeless mother, at age 21. Five months later, she was put on bed rest until she could give birth. She lost her job. Now she had no income and two mouths to feed. Humbled by this experience, she finally came back to live with her mother in Asheville, leaving behind the independent life that she had known for seven years.

Initially, Danika thought that moving home was going to be a curse, but it was really a blessing, giving her the support she needed while building the resources necessary to grow. She was able to join WorkFirst through the Department of Social Services and take advantage of the program to graduate from the work-readiness class (ASPIRE) at the local community college. In the ASPIRE class, Danika heard about ABCCM *Our Circle*, where she could get additional work-readiness training, assistance with job search, and most importantly, loving support from Allies from the community and her Circles Coach to help her achieve her goals. She got a scholarship to begin certified nursing assistant (CNA) class and also joined *Our Circle*.

"ABCCM *Our Circle* has shown the real aspects of Christian love. The positivity that is around here is what I like," Danika says. "At Circles they don't categorize you by your financial state, but as the person you are. They are always giving a helping hand. They give you tough love or the push you need... It's like walking into a family reunion versus a courtroom with a million stares and fingers pointing at you." Coming into the program with a misdemeanor larceny charge, Danika was afraid people would judge her.

"People sometimes label me as a thief. I am not a thief. I made a dumb decision when I was 17," she explains. She adds that the way the *Our Circle*'s "work-readiness" class was taught gave her a chance to "be real" and to get connected with her Coach and Allies, adding, "That helped me trust."

Since graduating from the Circles training, Danika has eagerly built relationships with her matched Allies to help her overcome obstacles to her ultimate goal of becoming a registered nurse. "Each Ally is a piece of the puzzle," she says thoughtfully. "Tom (Ally #1) used his network to reach out to contacts at Mission Hospital to try to help me get a job. Vera (Ally #2) helped critique my resume. Andy (Ally #3) has always been supportive any time I needed someone to talk to. They were all there for me when I had difficult personal matters. They text and check up on me regularly, which I really like. I really feel like they have adopted me and my daughter, A'Miya."

Having that relational support has helped her achieve her first goal. In the midst of a personal crisis, with her Allies contacting her daily to encourage her, she passed her clinical exam with the highest score in the class! A few weeks later, when she aced the national exam and got her CNA, her Allies and Coach celebrated her at a Circles community meeting with an award, a cake, balloons and a card.

Danika's Our Circles celebration

"It's been hard, but I am making it!" she beamed. Since then she has gone from part-time status to full-time and has been promoted several times. Danika has also realized another goal – moving into her own place once again.

In recognition of her hard work, dedication and accomplishments, Circles rewarded Danika with a car as a Christmas present. ABCCM had received the car as a donation, and *Our Circle* deemed Danika a very worthy recipient who has proven she is now capable of maintaining the automobile, required insurance and property taxes.

Danika is proof that the support of Circles and increased resources can lead to success.

Startricia and her son, also from Circles in Asheville, NC

Overcoming Generational Poverty
By Jennifer Lindberg, Pagosa Springs, Colorado

My name is Jennifer Lindberg and I was born and raised in Pagosa Springs, Colorado. Actually, I am a fifth generation resident of Pagosa Springs. My parents were just teenagers when I was born and they were forced by their parents to marry when my mother got pregnant with my brother. There was little opportunity here in Pagosa and my father decided that selling drugs was his best option. I don't really remember him having a regular job until I was in elementary school. My mom worked hard at any job that she could get as a high school dropout, like cleaning rooms and working at restaurants and gas stations. She had to make sure that we had whatever we needed because my father did more drugs than he was able to sell as a drug dealer. He was abusive to my mother and violence was a big part of our everyday life. My mother tried hard to make her situation better by getting her GED and going to a vocational school to become a bookkeeper. She would leave my father, and as most abused women do, she returned to him. We

25

lived like this for 18 years until I was a senior in high school and my mom decided she had had enough.

It would be great to tell you that my story was that of a girl who rises up out of the ashes and makes a new life for herself, but that wasn't the case. The trauma of my childhood haunted me for years. Although I did graduate from high school, I had no expectations of ever leaving Pagosa or making a better life for myself. I was very promiscuous, had very low self-esteem, and was pregnant by the time I was 19. For me, sex equated to love, and I needed to be loved. I worked as a waitress, cook, and many other minimum wage jobs. Finally, I decided I wanted more so I worked hard on getting new skills and I got a job as a secretary. I had hit the big time and was able to start working my way up to the middle class!

I was able to apply to purchase a home for my growing family through a program called Colorado Housing (similar to Habitat for Humanity). During this time, I met a wonderful man who was also from generational poverty, and we married. We moved into our home and started a new life. Like so many of us, we were told that all you have to do to be in the middle class was have a home, a nice car, and decent jobs. He worked in construction and he was making decent money. Neither one of us had the tools or skills to maintain a "middle-class lifestyle."

Soon after we moved into our home, we received some credit cards and refinanced our house to buy a brand new minivan to accommodate our expanding family. My husband's demons started to surface and the ever-growing pressure to "keep up with the Joneses" led to him to use the only coping skill he had, alcohol. He drank and I believed this was the way life was supposed to be. He and I both believed that filling our life with chaos and drama was "normal" since no one ever taught us anything different. We spent every penny we had and never saved for the future. We dug a huge hole and no one was trying to reach down and pull us out. Luckily, my husband was strong and he got sober (has been for eight years now!) and both of us were able to overcome some of the trauma through therapy. Unfortunately, we had dug ourselves into a deep financial hole. We had a huge mountain of debt, a mortgage we could not afford, and four kids to feed. My husband wasn't working full-time and I had to stay home because we could not afford daycare.

The cycle of poverty had caught up with us. We just didn't have tools in our toolbox to deal with living in a middle-class world. The psychological toll of growing up in poverty and violence was starting to catch up to us as well. We were emotionally unhealthy and living in chaos. As many people do when they are struggling, we walked into the sanctuary of a church, Community United Methodist Church (CUMC). We had been to church before, but this time it was different.

We started attending church because our boys were in Boy Scouts and the meetings were held at CUMC. We were searching for something, but did not know what it was. When a mom from Boy Scouts invited us to church, it felt right. We had been inside the walls of this church many times and what stood out was that there was always someone there who was helping others. We started coming to church and we built a relationship with Pastor Don Ford.

Coming to CUMC and meeting Pastor Don was a life-changing event for my family and me. Pastor Don made us feel welcomed to his middle-class church. He saw us for who we really were. Even when I felt like I was a poor person pretending to be in the middle class, he reassured me that I was never alone and that God's gifts were for everyone – no matter what your past held. Pastor Don has a reputation here in Pagosa for his incredible outreach in our community and as a community champion for people on the fringe of society. The church not only had a substantial food pantry that did not discriminate – if you needed food all you had to do was ask, but he had worked with community leaders from different churches, government agencies, and local non-profits to form Pagosa Outreach Connection (POC). POC provided assistance for people who just needed a hand up with assistance with anything from rent to utilities to day care expenses. He was truly living his beliefs and every time I came into the walls of the church, I saw people doing God's work. My family and I felt welcomed.

Before Circles, I had Pastor Don Ford. He was, as I have learned, my Ally. He did for me what Circles does for others. He built an intentional relationship with my family and me. He listened without judgment and never once told me what to do. He asked a lot of questions, he made me think, and he gave me some tools and skills to make the changes in my life. The number one thing that he did for me was he expected me to do better for myself. What changed me is that I actually had someone who expected me to do better and believed that I could and he never gave up on me. I was so used to people giving up on me that I tested his loyalty, a lot. He never walked away. I continue to be on the journey out of poverty. We have had many successes, and also failures, on this journey.

Three years ago, CUMC had the opportunity to bring Circles to our community. Pastor Don thought we might be a good fit for this program. We thought maybe we could just help others. It became much more than that. There were many tools and skills taught that we still needed help with as we gained more social capital. Through that process, my husband and I became more involved to the point of having a leadership role. When the opportunity came that the program was in need of a coordinator, my biggest Ally, Pastor Don, believed that I could do the job.

Every week I am able to give back the gift that was given to me. Circles of Pagosa Springs has 50-60 Circle Leaders, Allies, and children coming every week. We have been able to establish a reputation for getting results and changing lives. Many of our victories come when someone is able to pay their electric bill on time or get a job. When people ask us what Circles is, my first response is, "It's about relationships." Through new relationships, we can heal the past and move towards a new life.

My husband and I have come a long way since we started going to church five years ago and started Circles two years ago. We sold our house and became financially stable, debt free, and even have savings. Our oldest son is graduating from high school this year and will be the first in our family to go to college. He wants to be a history teacher. Our story is not finished yet. Circles changed us and changed our family. We are proof that it works.

Chapter 4: Why Community Programs Adopt Circles

Circles and Community Action
By Megan Shreve, Executive Director of South Central Community Action Circles in Franklin and Adams Counties, Pennsylvania

Megan Shreve runs a Community Action agency in central Pennsylvania. Community Action was charged with the original federal mandate from 1964 to "end poverty." Most community action agencies are managing specific programs aimed at alleviating aspects of poverty, but do not have the funding to focus on helping people out of poverty or to move their communities toward making a strong commitment to end poverty. Megan, however, has used Circles to leverage a critical dialogue in her community about the importance of making the conditions right for people to move out of poverty and into economic stability.

As I sit in the audience of a community meeting, watching Circle Leaders share their stories, I am once again astounded, not only at the poise and expertise shown by these brave families, but at the changes that have been made in our communities. They have given time and energy not only to improving their own situations but also to building a real path out of poverty for those who come after them. The phrase standing on the shoulders of giants comes to mind – we see more and see farther because we now see not only with our own eyes, but the eyes of those living in poverty and working so hard to get out.

Their faces and stories come flooding back. Each life so poignant and meaningful and far more complex than the simple stereotypes people assign. Becky, who spent nine months living in a campground because she couldn't afford rent, was walking miles to work when she had no car – not a lazy bone in her body. She convinced her young son that they were on an adventure so it would be easier for him. Now in safe, stable housing, she has been able to find full-time work, is building a secure future, and young William is thriving!

Or Roberta, a victim of domestic violence, trying to rebuild her life for herself and her children. She came to Circles, unemployed and not sure where to turn, but determined to build a new future. Her soon-to-be husband, Bobby, a giant teddy bear, told me Circles taught him not to be a taker – something the prison system failed at several times. They will proudly tell you how they have rebuilt their lives and rebuilt a dilapidated old trailer into a safe secure home, little by little. Now self-sufficient, they share their story with anyone who will listen and are taking classes so they can teach budgeting and finance to other families.

Two other success stories involve Shannon, her face bearing the scars of a serious car accident and her soul bearing scars as well. Her husband Edwin, who came to this country to support his aging parents – his Allies tell me he is the kindest, hardest working man they know. Evicted the week before they graduated from Getting Ahead classes, and yet, they kept pushing forward to build a better tomorrow. And they have done that. He obtained certification to do asbestos removal and has embarked on a new career, and Shannon, now working, serves on the Guiding Coalition helping steer the Circles initiative to help other families and change the community.

I think of Cara, the first Circle Leader in our Adams County Circles initiative to become self-sufficient and the story behind the Wage Gap video that has been shared nationally. This woman taught me real courage and helped me understand more about poverty than 18 years in the industry ever did. She worked hard, beat the odds, and now educates our community on ways to help create a path out of poverty. She has probably participated in more than 60 speaking engagements in the community. Not only does Cara work 70 hours per week managing a restaurant, she has made time to serve as Nereida's Ally – helped Nereida achieve her dreams and goals. And when Nereida, a victim of domestic violence, who now works for victim services in the courtroom, graduated and achieved her goals, she began serving as Becky's Ally. Circle Leaders becoming Allies and helping another family receive the support that helped them on their journey is what inspires me.

I see those faces and so many others as I reflect on my years of working with Circles. The strength of these families, the grit and determination to not only build a better future for themselves and their families, but to change systems and the hearts of those around them, is astounding and inspiring. How has Circles changed me? It has impacted everything about the way I do business and changed so much about the way I live my life.

I had worked for South Central Community Action Programs, Inc. (SCCAP) in Pennsylvania for 14 years before leaving the non-profit world to go into consulting. I did business process analysis, implementation, and training on large change management projects for a prestigious consulting firm. It was interesting, thought provoking work, I learned a great deal and honed my skills, and the money was great. But I really missed community work. Four years later, a board member from my old agency called to see if I was interested in applying for the executive director's position. After much deliberation and a family meeting, I sent in my resume. After a long interview process, I was hired.

I came back to the agency and found the same people, in the same rooms, meeting about the same things. Not much had changed, except we were serving more families with less money. No one was getting out of poverty. Don't get me wrong – we were doing good, important work, we were helping people remain stable and not fall off the cliff, but no one was moving out of poverty. And I have to be honest – that scared me. That business paradigm, serving more families with less money, can't continue forever and I certainly didn't want the wheels to fall off the cart on my watch.

We began looking for programs that helped families actually move out of poverty and while at a Pennsylvania Community Action Conference, I heard Scott Miller speak about Circles. I was completely intrigued. The model made so much sense! Scott took some time to meet with me and sent me lots of information. Then I took trips out to see two Circles sites in action and was astounded. I loved hearing from the Allies and the community groups, but what was most amazing to me was the engagement and advocacy on the part of Circle Leaders. They didn't see themselves as victims, but as people engaged in their own life and in finding broader-based solutions to help others. The experience was life changing. We signed a contract and our Circles journey began.

Because we had very little funding and because I wanted to experience the process, I facilitated the first two Circles groups in each county and served as an Ally for a family. I have worked in this business a long time. I have met with and provided services to thousands of individuals. But I never walked alongside them in the fashion that Circles facilitates. I never had the privilege of having them teach me about poverty, or took the time to encourage and listen to families talk about the issues, their experiences and the logic behind their decisions. And, though I intellectually knew that benefits ended before a family could afford to lose them, I had never seen that experience in such a first-hand manner.

It was impossible to stay passive or quiet after walking alongside someone as they actively work to improve their lives. You see the system sabotage their journey. On top of that, imagine having everyone around you assume that it is entirely your own fault and you are simply not doing enough. You begin to ask yourself, how much is enough? And nowhere else in the social services world do we truly engage families, who understand poverty far better than any of us, in finding and implementing solutions. Circles brings all of us to the table, we all share our gifts and talents, we all listen and learn, and we take action. And the world shifts.

As we watched Cara, the first Circle Leader in our initiative who became self-sufficient, we could clearly see the barriers that existed. When she took on a semi-professional job while continuing to waitress, she lost nearly all her benefits, including access to food stamps, and only had $20.00 to spend on food for the month. Not because she wasn't budgeting – she budgets better than anyone I know. One of our Allies, Dora, was talking about the frustrations of this with her friend who runs the farmers markets in our town, and the market began donating what was left over after the market to our families. Our first community solution was born.

Members of Adams County Circles

As that first group of Circle Leaders progressed, they invited Toastmasters to come and teach them how to speak in public (and when I say they, I mean it. The group of families decided on inviting them in and made the contacts.) That group, and others since then, have shared their stories at more than 60 venues from college classrooms, to panels after poverty simulations, to community forums on food access, to meetings with schoolteachers and principals, to statewide conferences. Their stories, as told by them, have been instrumental in seeing changes take place around us.

From their work on food access, a host of community solutions was born. It started slowly, with the local farmers market donating the food left at the end of the market to our Circles families. But over time, a food policy council was started, looking at the larger impact of food access and buying locally. Our farmers markets now have EBT and debit machines. We double the dollars of purchases made with SNAP benefits, opening this market to lower income families, which provides them with healthy foods and bolsters local industry. And one of the biggest impacts, The Gleaning Project, brought in more than 57,000 pounds of fresh fruits and vegetables, all harvested by volunteers at more than 29 farms and provided to low-income families. These are just some of our examples as they relate to food access. We have worked on issues related to education, health care, and teen parents, as well. Families, Allies and the community are working together to enact solutions.

We believe it is incredibly important to focus not only on the micro level of Circles – the families we are working with. That is a relatively small number. It could be five, 15, 25 or 100. But the truth is, there are thousands of families behind them. It is critical to work also at the macro level: what are we doing with what we are learning? Whether it is about food access, or educational inequality, the wage gap and the lack of a path out of poverty, what are we learning and what are we sharing with the community? And just as important, are we doing it in a way that invites everyone to the solution table?

This is part of the magic of Circles, it isn't low-income families in one corner and everyone else coming up with the solutions. It isn't doing for, it is doing together. It is hearing from families and walking alongside them. Seeing, really seeing, their experiences and then using what we are learning about poverty, about the choices we all make, about systems that are broken, about cultures, about the good, the bad and the ugly. It is about identifying, implementing and celebrating what works and exposing what is broken, talking about it honestly and then engaging the community to help us find solutions.

This work is brilliant. It is invigorating and strategic. It is tough and messy, and wonderful. It reminds us that together we can do so much more than we ever thought possible!

Weekly Circles dinner in Adams County

Circles and Housing
By David Harris, Volunteer Champion for Circles
Palmyra (Pennsylvania)

Three years ago, a friend invited me to a Circles meeting, a neighboring county's gathering for a Big View meeting. I left that meeting both exhilarated and puzzled. I was exhilarated by the relationships surrounded by tested helping principles, and a mission to help families and their communities thrive. And yet, I was puzzled because everything was so new to me: the Circles language, the possible applications, and the choices for our own community. When we left, I was eager to find out more.

Palmyra Circle Leaders and Allies

My name is Dave. I am a husband, father, musician, explorer, grandfather, community leader and person of faith. My own history led me to that exhilarating intersection I encountered at that first Circles experience. I was raised in a justice-oriented preacher's family in the 1960s. I was immersed in both inner city and rural outreach to help people. I was called to be a pastor. My journey has taken me to Kenya, Haiti, Lakota and Mohawk communities, the barrios of Juarez, Mexico, the hills of Appalachia, and to community and life development in the neighborhoods where I live and work. In short, I have a passion to make a difference in the lives of others.

Like others who share that passion, I've experienced my share of roadblocks, failed efforts, and personal frustration, along with the rush of success. The transformation stories and measurable results of Circles have captured my attention and stirred my imagination. I now live in Palmyra, Pennsylvania and work with the Palmyra Circles Initiative in that community.

When I moved here a decade ago, I met a mini-market worker who introduced me to the poverty and housing needs of my new town. Often homeless, she was "renting" unfinished space in her ex-husband's basement for herself, her daughter and her granddaughter – no rental agreement, no standard of safety and most of all, no security day by day. I was perplexed that other middle-class people in our community had not noticed the injustices that were shouting for my attention. Or perhaps, like many, they assumed these families suffered the consequences of their own poor choices.

These observations began my journey of helping people who were in poverty in my community of Palmyra. I initially served people directly by providing them with immediate relief services. I then moved into leadership roles on the board of our local Ministerium, the Palmyra food pantry, and as founder of a new affordable housing organization. These efforts, however, were not connected to a coordinated system of community supports. My interest in changing the whole community was peaking just as I was introduced to Circles.

There was no question of my commitment to be a part of bringing Circles to our area. My wife, Penny, and a friend, Lee, and I attended the Circles hands-on training program. I loved being a part of the supportive and creative leadership team that we formed to start Circles in Palmyra. I was energized by the possibilities of building a simple, replicable and effective system of supporting families and strengthening our neighborhoods for a better future. As my involvement grew, so did my personal investment.

The hours I spent in developing Circles broadened my networking and development skills. My life became less compartmentalized. No longer was I just a pastor here, a business association member there, and a parent in the school. My interest in Circles created a larger common purpose for the wellbeing of our town, and helped me to pull all of my community roles into one common effort. Through this new community building work, my contributions were being multiplied and coordinated in ways I never anticipated.

Part of the joy of Circles is celebrating the growth and changes I've witnessed happening with both Circle Leaders and Allies. August is a young adult who became an intern as a part of his college studies. I watched August build his community-building skills and professional social service repertoire. He was fired up by the new thoughtful connections he was making with adults, kids and the whole Circles effort. August worked diligently and creatively as we planned our start-up and was instrumental in organizing our child-care. August has since moved from the community but he has stayed connected to Circles and remains a personal friend.

Gail began, as many of us did, with middle-class expectations of efficiency and results. Her early frustrations as an Ally in a challenging situation were transformed into a wonderful asset for Circles. At the point that she was ready to give up on a Circle Leader situation, she turned to our Circles coach who advised her to change her role in Circles. Gail decided to use her administrative skill and personal warmth to organize an interview process for Circle Leaders in order to collect reporting data necessary for the program. In this role, she was able to offer her enthusiastic support to both Allies and Circle Leaders. Gail went from being a frustrated Ally who was unsure of how she could help to being a passionate supporter, excited to share her gifts.

Our business Allies provide vital resources for Palmyra Circles. Metz Catering, Brunos Subs, 3 J's Coffee, the Filling Station, Today's Chef, and Lebanon Valley College not only made food for 30-50 people a week a reality, but they provided computers for our Circle Leader families, gave resume and tax return help, and provided training resources. When we started, we didn't know if anyone would step up. Now, we have an abundance of support from our business community. Wow!

We have seen local legislators transition from a passive interest in the problems of poverty to becoming active advocates. We built connections with a state legislator, U.S. Congressman and state welfare official through informal community events and coffee. We then invited them to a formal legislative listening event where nine officials came to our weekly Circles meeting to hear the perspective that our Circle Leaders and Allies had on the problems of poverty in our community.

Most important are the changes experienced by our Circle Leaders. In our first Circles class, people were filled with uncertainties and their trust levels were low. Circles had no track record yet and our relationships with them were just beginning.

We are now preparing for our second class. One Circle Leader, Vicki, was very quiet when we met her. Now she is willing to speak up for herself and others. Vicki not only spoke at our legislative listening event, but she has spoken at the Circles Guiding Coalition's strategic planning day. Vicki is now using her newfound boldness as a building block to achieving her life goals.

Palmyra Circle Leader Tony Keller and Allies Rozella Wagner, Jan Glatfelter, and Gwen Pavasco

Wanda speaks passionately about how the Circles community and weekly meetings have helped her no longer to feel alone. Her son Zach was reluctant to attend at first. Now Zach is an active, contributing part of the group. Wanda set a goal to move up at work and shortly thereafter, we celebrated Wanda's new supervisory job.

The success stories continue to grow. There's J.P.'s rise from jail to marriage and a supervisory position at work, and the growth of

Michael's contracting business. The kids in Circles are learning about character from the leadership of three young college students studying to serve. Circles is not magic. Getting started takes hard work, boldness, and flexibility. Circles is an effective way to work on the long-term goal of eliminating poverty through individualized support and transformation. It requires honest learning from everyone involved. In its own wonderful ways, it allows for fun and friendship to occur in ways that are frequently missing from more clinical or task-based models.

If Circles tugs at your heart, know that it is a different approach. It is not a paternalistic program but rather an approach that is built on partnerships of mutual respect. It is driven by the goals and strategies of Circles Leaders. It does not keep a clinical separation between providers and recipients of services. It isn't driven by political affiliations, but rather it collaborates with all those who serve the public. Circles does not compete with other helping services. It partners with all who are at work in the community to address the problems of poverty. Circles doesn't "fix the poor," but engages the entire community in learning and development. Circles is not rigid, but rather it is a flexible community of relationships where everybody gives and everybody gets. Based on my experience, Circles challenges and changes everyone involved for the better. What a great adventure!

Circles and "Middletown USA"
By Molly Flodder, Executive Director
TEAMwork for Quality Living, Delaware County Circles, Indiana

It was 2001. Our community, Muncie, Indiana, was a finalist in the National Civic League's "All America City" competition. We had 70 people in our delegation at the Atlanta event, and we had just run our "dogs" and "ponies" through their paces to prove what a wonderful, hardworking, collaborative community we all lived in.

Then came a judge's last question: "I see here from your demographics that you have a high incidence of poverty. What are you doing – collectively, as a community – to reduce it?"

That was the beginning. We stabbed at an answer by talking about some specific after school and arts programs for low-income children and the like, but none of those initiatives were really connected. Nor did our community have any kind of plan to end poverty. Ending poverty was not an imperative for Delaware County. And that bothered me for years.

In 2004, the township trustee of the largest township in our small city of 70,000 located smack in the heart of the manufacturing rust belt, encouraged me and our organization, TEAMwork for Quality Living, to work together to do something about this need to address poverty in a collaborative fashion. (For anyone who doesn't know, Indiana is one of the last vestiges of the "trustee system" of poor relief.) We convened a team to help us, started with a poverty summit and tackled the "why" it was important to our community, startling the leaders with the extent to which local people suffered from lack of resources.

So we had some initial attention. Next, we needed to find a model where somebody somewhere was doing something about it. We looked up "poverty best practices" on the Internet and "eliminating poverty" kept coming up. We wanted to talk to these people from Ames, Iowa, who were aspiring to eliminate poverty and, in the fall of 2005, we brought Circles' Scott Miller and his colleague to town.

The rest is history, as they say. Our then nine-year-old grassroots organization that brought together volunteers in their quest to build a stronger community really began to look hard at the issue of poverty, realizing that its presence was a deterrent to every project TEAMwork had ever done and every strategy our community would ever create. Through the Circles model, we found we were on to something, and we began to shed many of our past projects to focus nearly full-time on this important work.

We officially began Circles in March of 2007 and are now one of the more seasoned initiatives around the country. We had knowledge of some success in Iowa and elsewhere, a few training tools, and a lot of enthusiasm. And little by little, we started our uphill climb.

It was and continues to be uphill. Just because some people in the community learned a little about poverty, it didn't mean they were interested in doing much about it. After all, isn't that why people pay taxes – to help pay for the food, shelter, clothing, transportation, childcare of those "poor people"? And why should some new group tap into scarce resources to do things "a new way" when there were beloved agencies who had been serving the poor for decades?

Two things became very clear to us. First, Circles offered lots of help and some structure, but it was not a "cookie cutter" approach. Muncie, Indiana, in spite of being called Middletown USA by sociologists since the 1920s, was unique. We surely didn't want to have to adhere to too many rules!

The second reality was that in spite of building relationships, if all we did was help one person, one family at a time, we would never move the poverty indicator needle. All we would be doing is running yet another case-management program. All we would be is a social service agency with another program.

And so, it occurred to us early that Circles couldn't run on a monorail. It was going to have to have a parallel track, or our vehicle transporting people out of poverty would fall over. That parallel track running alongside the one building relationships and intentional friendships with people in poverty was essential: community engagement. In short, what it meant was that if we were going to teach people to fish, we needed the community to help stock the pond!

As a long-time public relations professional with a penchant for social justice and about two-thirds of the way into my career, I could really get excited about that! Mobilizing a whole community to embrace the notion that our city and county could not sustain itself while supporting the level of poverty we had! What a noble cause.

But how could that happen?

We a have few strikes against us. First, our grassroots organization's beginning macro focus on lots of volunteer-led projects over the years had caused confusion about who we were and what our mission was. (For the record, when the luster of a new approach wore off at the beginning of our organizational life, it became harder and harder to raise funds in the midst of that confusion.) But because of the Circles model, we began to rebuild, rebrand and move in a positive direction.

I'd be glossing over the monumental issue if I didn't tell you that from the beginning of our poverty work, until about 18 months ago, we were in and out of a proverbial financial swoon. But we had a strong organizational board, committed people on the guiding coalition, and a corps of committed volunteers – Circle Leaders and Allies – who wanted to see us be successful. And we had so much passion for the work, buoyed by the lessons and support of other Circles communities all over the country.

Dorica, Coordinator for Circles in Muncie, Indiana and Heather, national Circles trainer from Springfield, Ohio

One effort that pointed us toward financial success began when we created a "white paper," a position piece to spur people to think and to act. "Solutions to the Poverty Problem: Harnessing Social Capital to Build a Sustainable Community" was its title (find it at www.teamworkql.org), and we quoted many experts ranging from John McKnight and Robert Putnam to Circles' own Scott Miller.

Our Board chairman pointed out to me as I worked on this and assembled community thought leaders to receive the paper that it could be our "swan song." Sometime later, I saw the Ivy Priest quote that inspired me to think otherwise: "The world is round and the place that may seem like the end may only be the beginning." Our last mayor created a Muncie Action Plan (MAP), and raising people's awareness about poverty was part of it. We took that as a signal and in 2012 put together a coalition of 18 organizations to focus on 30 events in nine days that brought poverty to the attention of our county.

One part of that nine-day blitz was to distribute a 75-page book of stories about people in poverty and those who serve them. The book was written by writers who collected the stories and wrote them in the first person and, thus, faced poverty while walking in the shoes of those storytellers. That Facing Project (www.facingproject.com) has gone national, and two of our young professional Allies have created a template that is being used by communities facing all kinds of issues across the country.

Some people missed that 2012 nine-day blitz and asked us to do it again – longer. So in 2013 our organization was project manager for Poverty Awareness Year and coordinated more than 40 events with the help of a coalition of 43 agencies and organizations and 15 churches. The newspaper ran 20 guest editorials written by our group. They also said in a follow-up article that we "preached to the choir" and we did. But among the nearly 500 different participants in community forums, town hall meetings, experiential sessions and informational events, we signed up a lot of new voices in the choir, too; and the momentum is growing.

Other ways to engage our community have included poverty simulations – a total of 74 since 2005 – and our augmented version of *Bridges Out of Poverty*: "Understanding People in Poverty" and "Serving People in Poverty."

A local bank made us the beneficiary of a huge fundraiser, raising $79,350 for us in late 2012. Their president was impressed with Circles, so we put him on our board. We became a United Way agency through an employment partnership with Work One, Indiana's workforce development coordinator. We are key players in many of Ball State University's efforts to build service learning in a community laboratory. We are partnering with churches, schools and other agencies. Our local congressman has even asked us to help him lead an effort to put the issue of the cliff effect in front of local elected officials and business leaders.

We are finding more and more that when people sit in community meetings to try to figure out how to "fix" things and solve problems, that TEAMwork and Circles comes up in many of the sessions as a tool, a solution. People want us to have resources and want us to keep providing the help that this model offers to people striving to become financially independent.

Are we the best kept secret in town? Not anymore. Are we a household name? No, not nearly, but that potential grows steadily.

We are a group of committed and transformed individuals who collectively make up a cause that is bigger than all of us. We help people build resources, reason and relationships. And even those people in poverty who do training with us but are never ready to be in a Circle are stronger, better, and realizing that there is a community of caring people that wants to see them be successful. And for those who can hang through their life tyrannies and move toward their self-defined finish lines, there is a respite from the fear, isolation, and frustration that poverty brings. For those middle-class members for whom paying taxes or writing a donation check is not enough, there is a safe place where they can encourage and hold accountable intentional friends who need a hand to hold.

Now, as I am within a few years of the end of my formal working career, I can look back and say that because of Circles, I am a different person and because of Circles, our community is becoming a different community. I am excited to be part of our work in Muncie, Indiana. I am delighted to coach communities in Indiana and Michigan as we play our ongoing role as a regional training center.

As players in the Circles movement, we are a part of reclaiming the role our forbearers played when everyone grabbed a tool and went to help the farmer rebuild his burned out barn. I am grateful for the opportunity to help lead this work. I am honored to be inspired by determined individuals and their encouraging supporters. Being in the "life-changing/community-sustaining" business is the best line of work any citizen of this world can ever have.

Circles and Workforce Development
By Tim Thorson, Former Director, Circles Wyoming

Government agencies also find that Circles helps to engage the community in ways that increase their results for those they serve. In Wyoming, Circles was started through major funding from the Department of Workforce Services.

A good friend who had recently been named to lead a community initiative to support families moving out of poverty introduced me to Circles. The initiative chose Circles as the model for this work. She was looking for board members who shared this vision but were open to a new way to approach the work. The idea of a new approach caught my attention. As a grant administrator, I funded a number of existing service providers in the community and had been frustrated to see that, despite the money and time directed at the problem, these services seemed to treat the symptoms, not the causes of poverty.

The more I learned about Circles – eventually succeeding my friend as executive director – the more I felt compelled to share this program in our community and with other communities. As I built relationships in Circles, I learned a new perspective on poverty and on wealth in our community.

How often, when confronting the costs of poverty, did I think, "I wish I could do something, but what can I do?" or, as when meeting a panhandler, "I want to help, but what if I just make things worse?" Like many, I wanted to make a difference but saw many of the community efforts not supporting lasting change. Having found something that actually worked – that had a rational foundation and enduring impacts – I had to be a part of it.

Having become part of a community that spanned economic classes and social backgrounds, I started asking different questions in my own circle of friends and peers. Better yet, I started to see my own connections in the community as conduits to introduce our Circle Leaders and Allies to decision-makers and influencers in our community. Instead of being the face of our organization, we had many faces. And these faces spoke with an honesty that no surrogate could match about their experiences in poverty and the changes our community needed to make.

We clearly need to make changes. Fifty years after the Great Society, the gap between the haves and have-nots is widening. Whether the solutions tried were mistakes or the mistake was not in doing more, now is a time for new solutions. The relationships at the core of Circles are what have always built communities. But in today's world, we need to deliberately create a Circles community where those relationships can be fostered.

Because Wyoming is a conservative state by most measures, traditional social services tend to get short shrift from our state government and community leaders. Ironically, this provided a clear field to try Circles and measure its impact. Our state leaders, including our governor and his family service and workforce cabinet members, have embraced Circles based on its results and the way we implemented Circles in our communities.

Circles is seen in our state as a way to support people on their way out of poverty. It is seen as a workforce and economic development tool, not, as many here rightly or wrongly see other anti-poverty efforts, as welfare. Circles Wyoming is not a gatekeeper to child subsidies, housing assistance, or other public benefit. By decoupling social support from economic support, we have the opportunity for both Allies and Circle Leaders to build friendships built on trust, rather than the carrot and stick often implicit in case management.

This lack of financial reward confuses some traditional funders. Organizations that want to see metrics in terms of services delivered, apartments financed or meals served require some education to understand how to measure the impact that Circles provides. Thankfully, the evidence of this impact is being measured in communities across the country. As this evidence is reviewed and reported, the challenge of explaining Circles is becoming easier.

This expanding base of evidence has also driven innovation within the Circles movement. Each Circles community can apply the model to meet their particular challenges. The results, collected from across the country and reviewed by academics and practitioners, has allowed Circles to identify and disseminate best practices throughout the movement.

Among the lessons we have learned in our Wyoming communities is that Circles works best in communities that already have basic coordination of community services. In communities without coordination between safety-net providers, Circles' staff ends up trying to bridge the divides between other services. Further, Circles may end up being seen as a stand-in for other public agencies rather than as an adjunct leveraging the work of these agencies.

Circles Wyoming weekly meeting

A corollary to this lesson is that without existing coordination, it is hard to get a consensus in the community to invest in bringing the Circles model to the community. This consensus is important in ensuring cooperation between existing providers and the group bringing Circles into the community. Particularly as Circles starts to change expectations among community leaders and funders, it is important for existing agencies to welcome these changes as the fruit of a team effort rather than feeling left out of the conversation.

Another lesson that we've learned is that the Circles model functions as a whole. Attempts to apply the ideas piecemeal tend to degenerate into either traditional social work efforts featuring agency theory of change and case management or traditional charity work characterized by a donor-recipient relationship rather than partnerships between equal humans with unequal resources working on their community's challenges.

We saw the greatest impacts in the lives of those Circle Leaders and Allies who became the most involved in the larger community issues – what we call our Big View Team. Our Circle Leaders made a positive impact – shifting the votes of several key legislators – towards expanding Medicaid coverage to include single adults. The Circle Leaders involved in this team built relationships with legislators and officials that they subsequently accessed in order to get more involved in other community issues. This empowerment of people from the middle class and poverty, a theoretical expectation, was played out in the lives of our volunteers and participants.

Inspired by my experience in Circles, I have chosen to return to school myself. As I start graduate school in public administration, my experiences in Circles resonate in every course. How can we get disproportionately under-represented groups involved in their community governance? How do we address issues of crime and unemployment? How do we find common ground in our work to improve the quality of life in our communities? Circles provides a path towards the answers to these pressing questions.

I look forward to staying involved as a volunteer with our local Circles community and to sharing the ideas of Circles with other professionals in my field. For me, and for many of the friends I have met through Circles, there is not really much of a choice. We have found a solution to many of the most intractable and difficult problems we face in our community. Now that we know how to solve these problems, how can we refuse the opportunity?

Circles and Neighborhood-Based Community Center
By Meg Olive, Columbus, Georgia (Open Door Community House)

Meg Olive works for a large community center in Columbus, Georgia. Her story about Circles reveals the changes that were brought about by offering people not only immediate assistance, but a long-term pathway to a stronger financial reality.

In 2010, the community center where I work decided to make some strategic changes in the way we served families. We wanted to change our ministries and programs from activities that only met basic needs to an approach that had the potential to make a long-term impact on the community. Instead of spreading our resources throughout the community in a thin manner, we wanted to make a deeper impact with families, even if that meant working with a drastically smaller number of people.

Meg (middle) and Circle Leaders at graduation: Tammy Bryson, Amy Smith, Cambreia Davis, Meg Olive, Dot Moore, Denise Cambridge, Adrienne Williams

Other agencies in our community began hosting speakers on the Circles program. We thought our piece of the work in the community would be to offer the initial classes and send our graduates into Circles at another agency. So we offered Getting Ahead classes for three years and found it to be very helpful in assisting and empowering people to create plans for change. But something was missing. The other agency in town did not implement Circles and we were not capable of supporting each individual in their work without adopting a case management approach, which we knew wasn't best. We also recognized the value of the focus on social capital that the Circles model offered, which allowed people to broaden their networks and make space for real change. So in 2012, we began implementing the Circles model in Columbus, Georgia.

I decided to stay and work with Circles because I saw the possibility for something new. Many programs have been operating in the same ways, using the same theories of change for years while the poverty rates in our communities climbed. It was going to take a new way of thinking about working with families to see real change. As someone who was raised in the middle class, I know how important relationships are for success. Who you know matters, and for families that only know other families in poverty, who they know is not going to help them get ahead.

Circles gives participants an opportunity (many for the first time) to make their own decisions about their work to move out of poverty. When participants begin to make the argument for change in their own lives, change is much more likely. Circles in our community is changing lives. We have participants who have returned to school to pursue further education or who have begun college for the first time. Participants have become more financially literate and have started spending and saving more wisely. Many participants begin to focus on their physical health – realizing that their bodies being healthy and strong is necessary to be able to work and care for their families. Participants have been able to work through conflict at their places of employment and maintain their employment thanks to new communication skills. Spirituality is something that several participants have found to be essential in their transition out of poverty and being able to strengthen their inner resources has been life changing.

In addition to the plans Circle Leaders have created for themselves, they are appreciating some of the smaller changes they have integrated as well. Families are learning what it is like to sit down and share a meal together at our weekly meetings so they begin doing this at home. Weekly meetings provide the opportunity for families to try new foods and healthier ways of preparing meals. Children and teens are encouraged to plan and build their resources through child development programming during weekly meetings. Circle Leaders learn what it feels like to be held accountable by someone who cares about them as a person and not just as a client.

Allies and volunteers are also changing as stereotypes are challenged, and assumptions about why "they do things that way" are being shattered. A deeper understanding of why families make the choices that they do is leading to changes in the ways Allies relate not only to families in our Circles initiative but to others in the community as well. Allies spent time riding the bus with Circle Leaders and realized how inadequate our public transportation system is. As a result, Allies formed new views on how they wanted their tax dollars spent. Our Circles community took part in the food stamp challenge and ate for one week on the average amount a food stamp recipient in our community receives. This was eye opening for many Allies and volunteers who now are paying more attention to what is happening nationally with changes to the food stamp program.

One Circle Leader asked specifically for a male Ally because she has teenage sons and she wanted them to have a male role model. That Ally is now teaching one of her sons to play guitar. As they sit together in his home and practice – in a part of town he normally would not have visited – change is happening. He also has taken the young man to performances and shows in our community and has expanded his social resources.

The president of our local university and his wife serve as Allies in our community. Their Circle Leader's children found themselves recently riding with the university president in the back of a convertible in the homecoming parade. Those elementary-aged girls can now tell you why college is important and higher education is something they see as an essential part of their future, thanks to this relationship and the hard work they see their mother doing as a college student herself.

One of our Circles, made up of people of different ages, races, and genders, regularly shares meals together in their homes. Recently they made meatloaf together and shared with one another how they keep up with their family budgets. These are only three examples of what is happening in our Matched Circles. As the coordinator of our Circles initiative, it is incredible to hear about the relationships forming and be able to see how that is leading to real and measurable change in peoples' lives.

Kim Jenkins, Susie Allison, Tammy Bryson, Tim Mescon

I have learned many things about Circles in the time we have been working to implement the model. We have found that *who people are* matters a great deal more than what they know when it comes to working with other people. The roles of staff in Circles are unique, and finding the right people who can build and manage the complex relationships with people from different backgrounds is essential and rewarding. I have also learned that there are people in our community who really do care and want to be involved – and they may not always come from the most likely places. We have had no trouble finding and recruiting Allies because we have been open to folks coming to us from any part of our community.

If we are asking people to make holistic changes in their lives to move their families out of poverty then we have to be able to provide them with holistic resources to help with every part of that change. We can underestimate how difficult the change will be for families moving out of poverty. Staff and volunteers will sometimes think that the changes in moving out of poverty are obviously beneficial and therefore easy to make. We are asking people to give up relationships with people who are important to them, even if temporarily, which can be very difficult.

We are also seeing the impact these changes are having on children of Circle Leaders. While most of the changes are positive in the long run, we have underestimated the impact of parents going to work, school, and spending money differently, etc., would have on the children now. Building in support for the kids and parents as these changes are happening is important.

I have also learned and appreciated that the Circles model is flexible and can be tweaked to fit your community. We have found ways to implement the model in our area that focus on the strengths of our community and help us work on our weaker areas. There are some things, however, that are non-negotiable and those things shouldn't be ignored. The networking opportunities across the Circles network are invaluable. The encouragement and support of those who are working to create the same kind of changes in their communities across the country makes us feel like we aren't alone as we celebrate and face challenges.

Before we started Circles in our community the director of our agency and I attended a Circles meeting in another state. I remember leaving the meeting that evening thinking, "I don't know how you do that. I don't know how you create that sense of community." What I have learned is that community is not something you can force – but something that evolves when people get together regularly and genuinely care about one another. Each week during our weekly meetings, I can look around the room and see nearly 70 people that now know people they would have never known without Circles. The spirit of community created by Circles helps us all see that *what benefits my neighbor ultimately benefits me as well.* We are all neighbors.

Being an Ally
By Angie Hampton, Columbus, Georgia

My husband and I became involved with Circles through a series of events in 2010. We were interested in assisting people who wanted to move out of poverty, and Circles was just forming in our community. We began as volunteers with the meals and childcare programs of the weekly meetings, eventually becoming Allies.

Our Circle got off to a little bit of a rough start because we found our Circle Leader closed off. She was self-reliant and busy. Her life as a single mother of three demanded this of her and she had become very independent, which sometimes translated to us as being aloof. Even though we were each struggling to connect, we all persisted. Gradually, over the course of several months things began to change. We shared meals, celebrated birthdays, holidays, attended her children's events, barbequed in our back yard and played card games like a big family. During this transition, our relationship grew and trust took root.

Although our Circle Leader was attending college classes and seemed to be making good decisions to improve her economic status, there continued to be a distance between us. Yet there was something very amazing that helped to bridge the gap and strengthen my bond with her. Our life paths were very similar. We shared the path of divorce, single motherhood and attending college later in life. Mistakes I had made long ago equipped me with experience and knowledge to draw from. As I started to share, I was able to provide her encouragement and insight as only someone who had walked in her shoes could do.

This culminated later in one life-changing Circle meeting when she suddenly, unexpectedly opened up. We had a breakthrough and had some very open discussion as a Circle. As we shared, two Allies talked about their experience with counseling to overcome feelings of insecurity and to learn to make better decisions. Through our resource connections, we made counseling available to her. She made the decision to give it a try. And she stuck with it. Over the next several months, we saw her blossom and her whole demeanor change. She became more confident, peaceful and engaged. It was wonderful to watch this metamorphosis.

It was then that we completely realized what Circles could do. We had been privileged participants in facilitating positive, lasting change for another person, her family, and hopefully, generations to come. It was personally meaningful and fulfilling to realize that my life history, both bad and good, was valuable for someone else. I found that the word "circle" describes not only the encircling of a family with "connections" and support but also a symbiotic circle where a new, lasting relationship can develop.

For anyone who contemplates becoming an Ally I would recommend patience from the outset. Those of us with professional lives are focused on results and return on investment. When you join a Circle, you are embarking on a miraculous journey. Circles can be a conduit for lasting change when each member of the Circle engages and persists. Give of yourself and you will be amazed at the outcome. Changing lives one family at a time.

Becoming a Circles Coordinator
By Shelly Martin, Salina, Kansas

I remember the day very well. It was a Sunday in early November of 2011. As my partner Ruth and I were just leaving our church services at Trinity United Methodist Church in Salina, Kansas, Pastor Carl Ellis and his wife Sandra, who led our Bible study class, approached us to invite us out to lunch. I could tell there was something urgent about this invitation. We met at a local buffet, and soon after we were seated, Carl and I were engaged in a casual conversation when all at once Carl asked, "Shelly tell me what you know about poverty in Salina." I was caught off guard. Poverty? Really? "Well, as an RN, I've worked with people in poverty at the hospital. But I wouldn't say I know a lot about poverty in our community."

"Well, let me ask you this," Carl continued. "How do you feel about working with people living in poverty?" For a moment, I didn't know how to answer. My experience was limited to the medical field, so I wasn't sure what to say. I was finally able tell him that I believed more needed to be done in our community to help families in poverty. "Perfect. Just what I needed to hear," he said. Little did I know that my journey into Circles was just beginning. Carl gave me Ruby Payne's book, "Bridges out of Poverty" and I was hooked. By February 2012, we were meeting with the director of the United Way, and Rodney Denholm, a certified credit counselor at the local Consumer Credit Counseling Services. We decided that we would try to bring the Circles model to the Saline County community. We knew with Rodney's counseling experience that he would be a great Coach. But how would I coordinate this program with no social service or community organization experience? I was scared to death of failing. My stress level was at the highest I'd felt for a long time, but I could not ignore the call. The tap on my shoulder was telling me I was supposed to do this. So, I said yes. Since that day, my life has been transformed right along with the individuals and families we serve.

As the Coordinator of Circles of the Heartland, I have felt blessed and stressed all at the same time. In July 2012, I attended the Circles USA training program and everything I thought I knew about poverty completely changed. I finally understood poverty in terms that I, as a nurse, could understand. It's a disease. Finally, I knew my mission. I grasped this idea and I still use it today to help my community understand poverty. I can show them that Circles is the medicine we use to treat it, and they are listening. We currently have over 60 volunteers that work with our 20 families and 34 children we see weekly. In two years, we have outgrown the first church we were meeting in every week. We have moved to the First Presbyterian Church where we have lots of room to grow even more.

The disease process of poverty needs to stop everywhere. With the growth of Circles I see happening in our community, I know that Circles is the cure we need to make poverty a thing of the past. So, to get that point across, I now go out and ask members of our community, "Tell me what you know about poverty in Salina." And they do. Thanks Carl.

Circles and Community Centers
By Suzanne Crawford, Boulder, Colorado (Boulder County Circles/Community Action Program)

In Boulder County, Colorado, there are three communities doing Circles: Boulder, Lafayette and Longmont. The County is the administrator and catalyst for engaging the broader community in Circles. They provided the national Circles movement to focus on eliminating the "cliff effects" that reduce critical subsidies like childcare and food stamps at rates faster than people earn new income to replace them. Suzanne Crawford, CEO of Sister Carmen Community Center in Lafayette, Colorado was able to get coverage on the cliff effects through a story by Brian Williams that aired on his program Rock Center.

When I first started my job as CEO of Sister Carmen nine years ago, it became apparent that we needed to do more for people who were living in poverty in our community. At that time, our main service was our food pantry. We also offered vouchers to our thrift store so people could get necessities for free. It quickly became obvious that it wasn't enough, so we expanded our services to include financial assistance and we started allowing people to come in more often for food. It still wasn't enough. The first few years I was here, we kept adding resources so we could offer more food and financial assistance. We weren't turning people away, and we were helping people stay in their homes and meet their basic needs. But we found it was difficult to actually help people move out of poverty.

Over the years, Sister Carmen Community Center went from an organization that was originally intended to help people with emergency situations to an ongoing source of support for many people in our community. Without our services, many people wouldn't be able to make ends meet. This realization caused us to start investigating ways that we might be able to help at least some of our participants move out of poverty, toward a greater degree of self-reliance. The Circles program is one of the ways we are doing that.

I first became involved in Circles after participating in Bridges Out of Poverty training, offered by Boulder County Community Services. That training was so interesting and helpful in my work that I became a trainer along with several other people throughout Boulder County. The goal was to educate people in our community about the causes of poverty and start a conversation about how to help people move out of poverty. Several organizations, including SCCC, then started offering Getting Ahead classes for our participants. Shortly thereafter, the Circles in Boulder County was started and SCCC joined.

I first got involved in Circles for professional reasons, as it seemed like the right direction for our agency. However, what has kept me involved is personal. I have been serving on our Big View Committee since its inception. Hearing the Circle Leaders' stories, learning about their challenges, and working with other team members to find solutions has become a passion of mine. I find it deeply satisfying to go beyond the surface and work on the underlying issues that are contributing to poverty in this country. In our Big View group, we've worked on everything from local issues like transportation to national issues like the cliff effect. And we've organized forums where the Circle Leaders can express their opinions and tell their stories to local and state officials. Watching people who previously felt disempowered find their voices and express their opinions leaves a deep, lasting impression.

What I love about Circles is that it truly does take a community to make this program successful. I love that it involves people from all walks of life in an effort to support people from their own community as they take steps to get out of poverty. I have seen the unlikeliest of alliances form between people who have vastly different political viewpoints when they realize that their ultimate goal is the same. Collaboration is not always easy. With all the different organizations and people involved in the program, challenges do arise. Ultimately, the time and effort is worth it when you see a Circle Leader reach a goal, like finding a job with a livable wage or finishing her education. Circles is proof that what Margaret Mead said is true, "A group of thoughtful, committed citizens really can change the world."

Circles and Young Parents
By Karen Burns, Circles for Davidson County, North Carolina

I am the Community Liaison for Circles in Davidson County, North Carolina. Our program is noteworthy because we received grant funding to offer Circles specifically to parents and expectant parents between the ages of 16 and 24. Thanks to that funding, coordinating and promoting our Circles community is my full-time job. When I was hired by our local family services agency to work with Circles, I was not familiar with the model. I was inspired to sign on because I had previously worked in the areas of mentoring and youth development and I loved the idea of building a community of support around young, struggling families in a rural county. What a great opportunity to use relationships to improve self-sufficiency and empower folks to change their community! Although I initially got involved for professional reasons, joining Circles has changed my sense of purpose and renewed my commitment to helping families succeed.

The service providers in our area have long underserved young parents living in Davidson County. Our Circle Leaders frequently do not finish high school and are unable to maintain jobs because of instability related to housing, childcare, and transportation. Safe and affordable housing is difficult to come by and the waitlists for childcare vouchers are long. The bus that serves our town does not run after 4 p.m. These barriers keep young people at home when they could otherwise be pursuing their educational or vocational goals. As a result, young families suffer from isolation as much as they suffer from financial insecurity. They are also cynical about the capacity of human service agencies to help them. In their eyes, no agency or system has stepped up to help them before, so why should they make another appointment or fill out more paperwork? Circles in Davidson County has become a trusted resource for young people who had previously given up on the idea that anyone would step up to help them out.

Like any Circles community, we focus on helping Circle Leaders develop the skills and confidence necessary to achieve their goals. We teach them how to plan, how to access community resources, and how to be a source of support to others. We work hard to recruit Allies from diverse social and professional networks so that Circle Leaders can expand their own connections in the county. Over the past two years, this project has resulted in some heartening success stories.

Dana began our program when she was juggling high school and parenthood. She is now pursuing a degree in nursing at a nearby college. Tiffany found Circles after fleeing an abusive relationship in another state. She earned her GED and is now living independently with her children. Tate was trading one fast food job for another and struggling to support his young family. His Ally works at the local community college and helped Tate enroll in a certificate program for welding. I look forward to the opening part of each weekly meeting where people share their "new & good" updates because I love to hear about the big and little victories that the Circle Leaders share with the community. Every step forward is commendable and we do not take any of them for granted.

It certainly feels good to know that Circles has helped many Davidson County families negotiate a path toward self-sufficiency. The most impactful part of our work, however, has been creating a safe space for young people to build community. As one can imagine, a young person who has experienced teen parenthood and severe poverty has likely been the victim of multiple traumatic experiences in his or her life.

Troy and Tiffany and their two children

Many come to Circles believing that no one else has seen what they have in life. *Who else could know what it feels like to be hungry? Or how scary it is to be evicted? Or how violating it feels to be abused by a family member? How can anyone else know what complete hopelessness feels like?* In our community, Circle Leaders find likeminded friends who can relate to the pain and isolation that they have felt. They validate each other's experiences and they work toward creating a safe space for each other. We trade isolation and judgment for fellowship and respect. We focus less on what we don't have and we focus instead on what we can give to others in the community. We hold each other's children and clear each other's dinner plates and give each other rides to work. We answer the phone when someone calls after business hours. For some Circle Leaders, this is the first reliable extended family they have ever had.

For those who wish to bring Circles to their own communities, I hope you do so with the understanding that this is unlike other curricula or programs you may have used in the past. It is not a workforce development program or a dropout prevention program. This is not a financial fitness program, either. While we certainly want our Circle Leaders to achieve any and all of these things, community comes first for us. This is not the same thing as serving dinner at a food pantry or trudging through another workbook. A successful

Circles initiative asks participants to assume a level of investment and care for others that might seem daunting at first. Once you begin to meet your neighbors, learn their stories, and watch them become leaders in a community where they might have previously felt like outsiders, you will wonder why you didn't start this work sooner.

Changing Minds, Changing Hearts
Conversation on a Train
By Marva Weigelt, Newton, Kansas

As I was returning to Newton from a Christmas visit to my family in Michigan, I ended up sharing a table in the dining car of the Southwest Chief with an elementary school teacher, a Coast Guard engineer from Virginia and a civil engineer from Seattle. I'm guessing we were all somewhere in our 50s and of a similar class background.

At first, I appreciated just listening quietly as the topic turned to the woman's frustrations with her job in elementary education and the specific role that "poor people" played in making her job difficult. A fair number of stereotypes and assumptions were shared on this topic before someone turned and asked me what I did for a living.

I aimed for a gentle delivery of the news that my work primarily involved the very segment of the population that had just been thoroughly marginalized and blamed for its own ills, as well as many of those in the educational system. I was interested in keeping open the opportunity to offer a different perspective.

How gratifying it was to begin describing the Circles model from my firsthand experience as an Ally and to sense in all three of my tablemates a genuine interest. Heads nodded. A number of thoughtful questions were asked. The teacher from Virginia fetched paper and pen from her purse to write down the web address for Circles USA so she could find out if there were any sites in her state.

Teresa's Circle: Jill, Teresa (Circle Leader), Cay and Marva.

Perhaps most encouraging of all was her emotional response. It was easy to see that her earlier stereotyping and dismissal were veils for her grief that there was so little hope of making a difference. "You're going to make me cry," she said, "Because there may actually be something I can do."

Chapter 5: Why Fund Circles?

Why I Invest In Circles
By TT Crosson, Pinedale, Wyoming

Circles has been supported by hundreds of people in positions at foundations, United Ways, government agencies, and by individuals with the means to make substantial gifts. TT Crosson helps administer her father's foundation while pursuing her own career in higher education marketing. She has been supporting Circles USA for the past three years with grant awards.

How did you first get involved in Circles?

I became interested in Circles by researching nonprofits that are making a difference in people's lives long term. Long term is the key. Throwing funding at a cause isn't enough; you need the human element to sustain success. I believe Circles provides that human element every day.

Why did you get involved?

My father created a family foundation a few years back that provided me with the opportunity to contribute additional dollars to nonprofits that specialized in assisting children and families in need. Prior to that, I basically donated what I could to nearby community nonprofits. With more funding, I was able to branch out and provide needed funding nationwide. My goal was to find a nonprofit that produced a rate of success long term and helped families who really wanted a better life for themselves and their children.

What changed for you by getting involved?

My family has always stressed that hard work pays off and that nothing is worth doing unless done well. From my experience, Circles also believes in that same lesson. It is not easy to provide guidance, leadership and support throughout the many cities, townships and neighborhoods that Circles' volunteers reach, but they do it and from their results, they do it well. My thought goes back to my family. I had wonderful grandparents and an aunt that were my support group. Everyone survives better in this world knowing they have someone to turn to for support. It is beneficial to know that you are not alone in this world. With Circles, no one has to be.

What changes did you see in others?

My experience stems from talking with other benefactors/donors and Scott Miller directly. Scott is passionate about eliminating poverty. In order to reach many you need to inspire many, and Scott does just that! My desire is to pass that inspiration on to other benefactors/donors as I network through the many organizations I deal with. So to answer the question, I see positive changes in myself and other benefactors as I communicate the cause, need and effect of Circles. It is rewarding to know that someone can do more than just donate money. Circles provides many ways to make a difference. Basically, it comes down to economics and human behavior, which is pretty simple stuff to communicate to an individual or an organization.

What have you learned about doing Circles that you think is important for others to know about as they get started?

As a member of a foundation, I believe the financial aspects and underlying results are why I continue to support an organization like Circles. Circles functions as an organization in high demand and continues to strive to meet the demand efficiently and effectively as they grow. I know our dollars are being used wisely and for a great cause.

What do you think are the primary "selling points" for getting involved in Circles?

The human aspect is so much greater with Circles, which comes from devoted volunteers, training and appropriate tools to work with in the communities. However, what most impresses me is the integrated data system that tracks results. Circles has the ability to track a variety of measurable outcomes, which is difficult for any organization, but especially for the nonprofit sector.

Again, from a financial aspect, if your goal or mission is to make the world a better place or to aid in resolving poverty by funding a nonprofit, you owe it to yourself to become involved in Circles. It is a great feeling to make a difference. As Circles continues to evolve, more money and human interest is required. This organization is worthy of your investment, dollar for dollar, and the returns are amazing!

What expectations should people have coming into Circles? What would you encourage them to consider, and what would you discourage people from thinking about as they contemplate getting involved?

Everything worthwhile takes time. Don't expect results over night if you want to address the complexities of poverty. Good work and results takes time.

New staff learning Circles at the Hands-On Training Program

Investing in Circles
By Carolyn Workman, Columbus, Ohio

Carolyn Workman has been a long-time financial supporter of Circles since our early years. She got involved on the ground floor with building Circles in her former hometown of Troy, Ohio.

I helped envision a Circles program in my community. We brought together key partners for both funding and participation, and I helped work out the details of the necessary components for a successful program. I solicited, interviewed, and trained both Circle Leaders and Allies. This program is about relationships and bringing stability to people who live in the constant turmoil of poverty. We followed a thoughtful timeline of necessary steps to begin our first Circles of Hope in 2007.

Having been a social worker with both schools and a non-profit organization, I was well aware of the challenges that face individuals struggling with poverty. And the struggles that face schools and agencies in helping these individuals were always filled with heartfelt attempts, short-term solutions, inadequate funding, and often, disappointing results. People remained in poverty, and continued to struggle. I was pleased to learn about this Circles approach, and very interested in learning that this program wasn't about "mentoring" or "doling out," but about learning together, bringing in resources, sharing, and growing. It was about helping people get OUT of poverty, and sustain that stability for themselves and their families.

It was exciting to see how eager the participants were, and how the Allies took to heart that the person in poverty is called the Circle Leader. Indeed, the Circle Leader was in charge of bringing his or her Circle together to achieve their personal goals, utilizing his or her own skills as well as the skills of the Allies.

Both Circle Leaders and Allies received thorough ongoing training and support. Establishing and presenting goals proved a challenge for Circle Leaders while listening skills and understanding poverty culture were challenging for Allies. Allies were humbled as they learned about the numerous issues that faced a family living in poverty. Circle Leaders slowly learned to trust their Allies, once they

66

knew that Allies had their best interests at heart. Allies passed along middle-class values regarding their work ethic and accountability. Over time, friendships and teamwork built upon true concern and caring were formed. People achieved successes step-by-step, including many steps backwards. Each victory and challenge was celebrated and embraced by the entire Circles community.

Until someone has been part of a Circle, they cannot understand the sacredness of true friendships, where all members hold a space of love and trust. Circles provided a real opportunity to lay aside judgments and to learn how to have patience and open-mindedness in order to support one another. I learned that problems are complex, and there is not just one way to accomplish something. It became very clear to me that the biggest gift to a Circle Leader is to be continually present. There is no need to rescue or to feel sorry, but simply to hold a supportive emotional space for people.

Circles enhanced the life of both my family and me through lessons of humility, trust, and open-minded relationship building. It is "what God has in mind" and allows so many people to live their lives more fully in a way that brings all of us more joy and satisfaction.

Circles meeting in Troy, Ohio

I continue to support Circles financially at the national level. In doing so, I have had the opportunity to learn about the challenges of bringing a good program to scale. National capacity building is critical to take Circles to an effective level. Generating and applying current data to sustain and grow Circles is important. Communities benefit when folks have a weekly program to come together and discuss local issues. As a key funder of Circles, I believe that my support can help make a significant difference. Preparing people to become employable and secure is important, and upholding healthy successful relationships benefits us all. I believe that Circles USA understands the full challenge, and provides an evolving model to bring about more stability and peace.

Starting Circles
By Karin VanZant, Springfield, Ohio

Karin VanZant started Circles in her own community back in 2006.

She and her colleagues at Think Tank, Inc. have provided Circles USA with strategic planning, consulting, curriculum development, training, coaching, and conference planning assistance. Karin has helped many communities get started with Circles and provides the following insights for anyone who is interested in bringing it to their own community.

There are several stakeholder groups involved in a successful Circles initiative. They come from various parts of the community with their own agendas and ideas about what needs to happen to address the issues of poverty. They are all committed to being a part of identifying the issues and, at various levels, a part of implementing the solutions. The individuals in these stakeholder groups are informed and active in a part of their silo but have limited access to other parts of the community. Circles is a model that allows these various stakeholder groups to convene, build relationships and address the most pressing issues in their community.

Many times when I am speaking to new communities about "why Circles" or "what is Circles," I help them to understand that Circles is a two-fold approach: outward and inward. There are parts of the model that focus on the *outward* relationships in the broader community that involve a wide variety of individuals from the most diverse backgrounds. There is also an *inward* focus to Circles that allows individuals to connect on a regular basis and build more intense relationships that will ultimately lead to a transformational experience for all involved. The outward focus includes stakeholders such as various funding institutions and leaders from various organizations focused on issues of poverty and economic development. The inward focus includes stakeholders such as volunteers who want to be exposed to the personal journey of poverty and those who are actually transcending poverty. In Circles, we refer to the volunteers as Allies and to those on the journey out of poverty as Circle Leaders. Regardless of which stakeholder group I am speaking to, they all want two questions answered, "Why should we engage in Circles?" and, "What role do I play?"

It would seem that there would be a very similar answer in response to these questions no matter who was asking. However, in Circles there are various levels of engagement for those in the community depending on whether you are a part of the outward or inward process. So let's explore what the differences are and how best to engage these various stakeholder groups.

Outward Process

The outward focus is the one I always engage first. These are the community leaders, organizational staff or community champions who want to make something different happen where they live. These are the front-runners who are tired of the same approach to addressing poverty and who are tired of seeing the same families falling through the cracks of the current structure. These are the folks who have attended a training, workshop or seminar and heard about the powerful work that Circles has done in other communities. These early adopters begin the research process to find out where and why this approach works and then reach out to Circles USA to begin the conversation of "how can we bring Circles to our community?" For these stakeholders to really engage in a robust conversation about Circles, I present to them the results from my own community as well as the data that has been tracked since 2008. I am able to talk about the 60-plus Circles sites that I have personally visited and relay the stories of Circle Leaders and Allies that I have met and how their lives have been transformed via building relationships, assessing resources and identifying the purpose in their lives. I challenge the community catalysts to dream with me about what it could be like in their community if the individuals and families who have always been on the bottom rung of the economic ladder could somehow find themselves climbing the ladder towards prosperity and a full quality of life. This is a 35,000-foot, big picture, pie-in-the-sky, and visionary conversation. I love these conversations because when you first start out, there is a sense that the problem takes up all of the space in the room, and by the end the focus has shifted to the possibility, the opportunities and hope. It is a beautiful thing when you can capture the imagination of community front-runners and help them to connect the dots on dreams they have been holding on to for years.

Consultant and Circles Ally Marlo Fox from Springfield, Ohio and Circles New Mexico Coordinator, Delma Madrigal from Albuquerque, New Mexico

Another stakeholder group that we engage early in the Circles conversation is with those who have financial resources and can assist to build the infrastructure of Circles. I have been in many meetings across the country talking to local governments, community foundations and social service organizations about the investment that it takes to begin Circles and sustain it. I find it ironic that some funders seem very comfortable supporting the same approaches that have been proven not to work. But for those who have a zest for something new, powerful and creative, Circles is right up their alley. Anytime I am ready to approach a funder or stakeholder that can help with building the foundation of Circles I do my homework. I engage in research to find out what drives the members of that organization. I suggest you take some time to see what the core value for the foundation is – not just what is published on their website, but what really makes the people in the foundation jump out of their seats. Then I suggest clearly linking that passion with the tangible results that Circles communities are experiencing.

Inward Approach

When working on the inward approach of Circles, amazing things begin to happen very quickly and before you know it, you are far past where you ever thought you could be. This was my experience in both Springfield and Dayton, Ohio where we started our first two Circles sites in 2007 and 2009 respectively. When I first heard about Circles, many of the issues I had faced as a person from situational poverty and as a social worker seemed to be answered. However, I knew what the Circles manual might say and what really happens are oftentimes two different things. I spent much of the next five years working at every level of our local initiatives and eventually at the national level. Springfield is a suburban community halfway between Dayton and Columbus. I have lived in this community my entire life and decided to raise my family here. However, Springfield had seen its share of hard times, many years before the official national recession hit, due to the strong ties to the manufacturing and trucking industries. With skyrocketing poverty, significant reductions in middle-class jobs and a failing school district, this was a perfect place to try something new. We began with our first class of Circle Leaders in June of 2007 and many of those families are still involved with Circles today, some as Allies, some as Guiding Coalition members and some as community Leaders. That first class showed us the power of the model and our first group of Allies proved that amazing things could happen if given the right tools, the right support and a lot of positive encouragement.

From that first class of Circle Leaders, we have a single mom who has earned her Associate's Degree, is debt free and her daughter is enrolled in the first graduating class at the STEM school. We have a couple that has gained employment, reduced over half of their medical debt and become community champions for Circles. We have story after story of ways the first 13 participants have impacted our community and how their success became a ripple of success for the next 11 classes in Clark County. Yes, we have had our share of challenges, and not every Circle Leader graduate has made significant improvement, but what we hear time and time again is that no matter how long a person stays in the initiative, they gain insights into their lives, their resources and their community that they never knew were there. It is these stories of personal success, of support, of overcoming barriers and of finding their voice, that help me to inspire others starting the process for themselves or for their community. I make sure to tell each person I coach or talk to that my life is forever changed because of this work. I can never go back to the social work or broken system I worked in prior to Circles because I now know what it takes to break the bondage of poverty – relationships.

Now that I have been an Ally twice since 2007, I can speak to the steps and fears that Allies have as they are going through training and the initial steps of being matched. Even as a professionally trained social worker, I was nervous about being matched. What would be expected of me? What if something happened that I couldn't handle? What if I did something wrong, said something wrong, let someone down? I knew it wouldn't be the end of the world and I knew that I wasn't alone, but these fears were very real and became strong the closer we got to the match meeting date.

Being an Ally is not difficult, but does require a foundation of awareness and understanding before beginning the process. I like to encourage potential Allies to complete the training, write reflections, read various books along the way and ask lots of questions. The more you ask, the more you know; the more you know, the more comfortable you will feel.

Both Circle Leaders and Allies are central to the DNA of any Circles community. The other stakeholders on the inward focus are the staff and volunteers. The best advice I give to staff is to make sure they are practicing everything they are teaching to Circle Leaders and Allies. Circles staff need to have their own Allies, their own assessments and especially, their own goals. They need to feel supported and replenished on a regular basis. Self-care, healthy boundaries and life balance are all a part of the keys to being a long-term, effective Circles staff member. Remember it is a marathon not a sprint.

As you can tell, I love this work. I have been transformed and have seen amazing people all over North America whose lives are better. I have heard story after story of success, of advocacy, of empowerment. I pray that those who are considering this work would reach out and become inspired to begin. Start now. Don't hold back.

Amazing things are waiting…

Members of the Ohio Circle Leader Council at the Annual Circles Conference: Tara Elyea, Stacy Carroll, Dee Baker, Joy Barnhill, Christina Tellis, Melissa Marshall

Finding My Story to Help Start Circles
by Jackie Volbrecht, Circles Marion County (Kansas)

Jackie Volbrecht helped start Circles in her hometown of Marion, Kansas. This is a wonderful story about "finding your story" to promote the purpose and value of Circles.

Destiny Cash, a Circle Leader from Marion County at the Kansas Circles Conference

That's not fair! I think that was the first sentence I ever put together and I would be wealthy if a nickel were deposited in the universal bank of complaints every time I issued this declaration.

I was programmed to this way of thinking and in Circles, we call that a lens. I see much of the world through my father's lens. I was taught that whenever I saw the word "public" I owned it, I should care for it and share it with others. I grew up with a huge stake in this world.

It was inevitable I would work towards making life fairer, that I would embrace the civil rights movement, help teach English to refugees, and stand by food carts in the grocery store collecting mostly beans.

Clothing drives and working on Habitat for Humanity houses kept me in the thick of things, yet fairness eluded me. What I spent so much of my time doing only relieved some symptoms of the terrible inequities I witnessed in the world. My efforts accomplished very little. Then, I heard about Circles and the more I heard about it, the more I thought, "This is it!" They said their work is intended to eradicate poverty. Eureka!

We are in a small rural Kansas community, having few resources, no Wal-Mart, no United Way, only our determination and hope. Rural poverty is mostly unseen and programs are directed by achieving the numbers. How many did you feed today?

Ultimately, the families here suffer greatly from lack, including a lack of services, lack of transportation and lack of access to low-income housing. I have visited homes where holes in the floor are covered with license plates, homes where electricity has been cut off for years, the lines and meters removed. The family heats and cooks on a wood-burning stove and they are forced to use railroad ties when all other sources are gone.

So we began with the hope of becoming a Circles site, knowing it would take something miraculous to obtain the funding to start.

Then, an act of God happened! A terrible windstorm took out trees, including one that fell on my car! The debris was everywhere and when it was gathered up into piles, it sparked an idea! Why not try to raise funds by setting a Guinness world record for the most people at a marshmallow roast?

We contacted my son, who works for a Chicago public radio station and is ever so talented. We asked him to design a shirt so that we could sell them to raise funding for Circles. We printed on them, "Marion County Lake, where marshmallows come home to roast!" It was a beautiful thing. The Governor even bought one of our shirts and we sold out!

Jackie Volbrecht and Linda Ogden, who is wearing the "Marion County - Where Marshmallows Come Home to Roast" shirt

We set the record and sold $6,000 worth of shirts, enough to make a deposit on our Circles future! We made a brochure and I began my "speaking tour" about Circles to churches, Kiwanis, ladies' book clubs, the Chamber of Commerce, and senior centers. Many of the organizations just needed a speaker to fill a luncheon spot. Some people listened, but few people "got it."

I was passionate and statistically sound about our poverty rates, but no movement was happening and a lot of stereotypical poverty stories were tossed back our way including "the person who took food bank food and sold it for drugs," "the person who sits around all day plotting on how to take advantage of our benevolence," etc.

I was fast losing heart, exhausted and ashamed that I was not able to communicate this world-changing vision. Then the answer to my communication problem literally fell in my lap. Well actually, it fell in the lake in front of my house! A frantic knocking on the front door caused my two dogs to jump straight up and fall off the couch. A young woman stood at my front door and shouted, "She fell in the lake! She's in the lake!" So me with my bad hip and my husband with his bad knees, together we hobbled as fast as we could across the road, following this stranger.

Sure enough, there she was, armpit deep in the water, wedged under a stairway that led to a floating dock. The young woman jumped in and I kicked off my shoes, ready to follow when reason prevailed. (Jackie, if you jump in, there will be two old ladies to pull out of the lake!) I assessed the situation and told the girl who was pushing on the woman to stop, at which point I observed she was older and overweight. I asked her if it felt like she was stuck. She told me she thought she was stuck in a hole. I asked if she could move her legs. She tried and the answer was yes. Then we began the process, inch by inch of getting her to move her legs so she could stand. Several times she moaned, "I can't do it!" I assured her she could. When she was able to try and stand, I put my hand on one of the steps and asked her if she could reach my hand. She could, so rung by rung, her hand on mine, she pulled herself up to standing.

I then talked her around to the stairway, up and out, behind her every step of the way while she was all wet and muddy and covered with lake slime. But we made it to the shore! I really have no idea how long this took, as I was so focused on the task, and as the astronauts say, failure was not an option!

How long should it take to get someone out of a lake? How do you measure your success? Simple, you succeed when she walks away.

She had been looking for her little dog but leaned too far before falling in. Is there any good reason for falling into a lake? Any reason so dumb that you would just say, "Well, that's what you deserve?" I didn't even get her name and she was too exhausted to even say thank you. But you know, that isn't why I did it.

There were no thoughts about fairness or equality, no questions about why she was there, no judgment on whether or not she had made a dumb mistake by falling in the first place! There were no thoughts about whether having pulled her out, would she jump back in. I had no thoughts about whose responsibility it was to help. No, it was what must be done. It was not an option to leave a lady stuck in the lake. It was the right thing to do and then the honesty of the moment just washed over me...It is the right thing to do.

Here was my story that encompassed everything that is Circles! I now end my presentations by looking my community in the eyes and telling them that 30% of Marion County has fallen into the lake and helping them to pull themselves out is the right thing to do.

And they are getting it!

What's The Research Say About Circles?
By Mary Jane Collier, Ph.D., University of New Mexico

The impact and success of the Circles program since 2000 has been researched numerous times over the past ten years by professors and students at Iowa State University, the Wilder Institute, University of Oregon, University of New Mexico and University of Michigan. These studies have confirmed that Circles is a comprehensive, long-term, holistic approach that uses components that are essential for supporting low-income women and men in becoming economically stable.

We have been working closely with Dr. Mary Jane Collier from the University of New Mexico on researching Circles and making changes to the programming based on what she and her team have found helpful and not so helpful in the field. Here is her account of Circles.

Sometimes we are fortunate enough to meet the right people at the right time and place. I met Scott Miller at a neighborhood association meeting in Albuquerque, New Mexico, promptly read his first book, and set up a meeting to ask more about the Circles model, research and evaluation. As we talked, I began to see, hear and feel the potential of Circles to move families to sustainable financial stability. I began to marvel at Scott's unwavering vision, his ability to explain the complex systems that produce poverty, his grasp of the impact of poverty on individual lives and communities, and his boundless energy. When Scott said an evaluation study might be very welcome, I was hooked!

I am an academic who has devoted her career to research and praxis about how to understand communication and cultural difference, how to work with conflict, and how to build relationships for social change. I am drawn to work with Circles because it is a flexible, long-term, community-based strategy for moving culturally diverse individuals out of poverty and for facilitating communities to take action on local systems policies and barriers to economic prosperity. Also, the core principles of the Circles framework are based on ethical practice and collaborative change. Participants moving out of poverty are viewed as the Leaders of their own lives; with support from community volunteers, Allies. Circle Leaders moving out of poverty form equitable and mutually beneficial relationships and share resources, and community members are responsible for working together to change system-wide barriers to economic stability. I also like that the framework is adaptable to local contexts and the needs of local cultural groups. For instance, across the U.S. the framework is being tailored to address regionally specific challenges such as generational poverty or high rates of unemployment and failing businesses, to include challenges being faced by racial and ethnic groups experiencing disproportionately high rates of poverty, such as African Americans in the deep South, or Latinos in the Southwest; or to meet the needs of such groups as military veterans and single mothers.

In 2011, Brandi Lawless, then a doctoral student at University of New Mexico, now a thriving assistant professor at the University of San Francisco, and I conducted a major formative evaluation study of Circles. We wanted to build on past research findings and quickly discovered that there were several previous evaluation studies. We found an evaluation study on 30 early participants by the Wilder Institute in 2008, and a University of Oregon assessment study in 2009 that offered an overall endorsement of the Circles model along with recommendations. An impact report in 2010 described that after only six months of involvement, there were dramatic increases in Circle Leader earned income and assets, clear decreases in welfare benefits, and major expansions in numbers of "people in my life who can be counted on." (Note that these trends continue to be evident in subsequent impact reports.)

I discovered several things that I wanted to understand better. For instance, the past research did not ask Circle Leaders and Allies how they felt about the training curriculum. Since the training curriculum at that time was produced by a national for-profit organization, and I had read some critiques of those materials as overlooking racial, ethnic and gender differences, I wanted to know how Circle Leaders from diverse racial and ethnic groups viewed the curriculum. I have also studied how racial, ethnic, gender and class differences can affect experiences of conflict, negotiation of identity positioning, status and resources, and the potential to form intercultural alliances. So I wondered how Allies who identified as white, middle class and male, for instance, and Circle Leaders who identified as African American and Latina/o and female, experienced their alliance relationships. Finally, I wanted to hear the views and experiences of Circle Leaders who had been involved for 18 months and beyond.

Tawana and Katie are Circle Leaders from Bloomington, Indiana

We decided to do a formative evaluation, which means we wanted to get first-hand views and experiences from various people affiliated with Circles and we wanted to use that information to guide decisions about what to keep and what to change. Brandi and I visited Circles sites across the U.S. and attended community of practice conferences and the national conference. We spoke with 90 Circle Leaders, coaches, Guiding Coalition members, Allies, volunteers, funders and national leadership team members. We wrote a summary report of our findings and included what everyone said was working and useful, what was less useful and challenging, and changes they recommended for the future.

We wrote a book chapter about all the diverse "dances" we moved through with different individuals, groups and organizations (Lawless & Collier, 2014)[1] We are collaborating on several other publications as well.

We learned that there was widespread agreement about how the current curriculum was a good conversation starter and laid some important groundwork. But overall there was a strong need to develop a Circles-specific training curriculum to include more about Circles as a framework, development of leadership, how to manage cultural stereotypes, how to develop cross-class Alliance relationships, and how to tackle Big View systems barriers. We learned that Circle Leaders who identified as African American and Latino/a, as single mothers, and those who lived in areas with histories of racism and discrimination did experience their cultural identities as being marginalized, and they didn't see these issues in the current curriculum. We also saw that Allies and Circle Leaders had some different views of what their relationships should be.

Therefore, we took the evaluation findings from our 2011 study and used them to guide Circle Leader and Ally training curriculum development. The National Evaluation Team coordinated a pilot study of this new curriculum, obtained feedback from Circle Leaders and coaches in selected sites and continued making refinements. In response to a need for reliable, valid data across the U.S., in 2013,

---

[1] Lawless, B. & Collier, M. J. (2014). Dancing in Circles®: Evaluating U.S. Community-Based Initiatives Moving Families Out Of Poverty. In Collier, M. J. Community Engagement and Intercultural Praxis: Dancing with Difference in Diverse Contexts (pp. 137-163). New York: Peter Lang.

Circles USA implemented a new national, online, integrated data system. This system stores Circle Leader progress report indicators related to income, debt, education and training, and social support at six-month intervals, as well as information on Big View actions, Ally participation, Guiding Coalition activities, and evaluations of the training curriculum. This data system enables Circle Leaders, coaches and Guiding Coalitions to have immediate access to data they need, to track their own progress, and to see evidence of outcomes being experienced. It also enables evaluators like me to assess short-term and long-term participation and outcomes.

Another reason that I continue my own involvement is that my evaluation work has been embraced and widely supported, and this includes having the support of the leadership team. Nonprofit organization leaders sometimes legitimately worry about what the "critical" evaluator will find and how feedback about what isn't working well will be shared. Scott, Brandi and I did develop agreements about how our documents and publications would be made public, and I did hear some voices saying they were happy with the status quo and were resistant to changes in the curriculum. However, I most often heard comments like, "We need to learn what is not working as well as what is working because we need to keep improving." "Everything is changing around us, the economy, federal policies like SNAP, and who is touched by poverty, so we need to be open to change, too." And, "Sometimes someone from the outside can learn more than we can on the inside."

In addition to so many appreciating the role of evaluation, my research has been a good experience for me because Circles meets my high standards of what a national anti-poverty initiative should try to be. First, I feel that the big picture context, systems and "structures" such as histories and experiences of communities and national, racial, ethnic, gender and class groups, and the role of institutions such as government agencies and their determination of poverty levels and policies about when certain resources are given or cut off, must be included in any strategy for moving families out of poverty. Some national programs and publications put the responsibility exclusively on individuals to move themselves out of poverty; this ignores the need for all of us to work to change systems that benefit some of us more than others, and to change policies and conditions that become barriers to achieving financial stability. For instance, federal policies are now in place such that acquisition of a minimum wage job means other forms of assistance are abruptly stopped, the "cliff effect," which often puts families into more debt; business practices by predatory lenders whose loans come with daily increases in interest rates are not monitored by city agencies; and city councils are not prioritizing affordable and safe housing.

Allies Daniel and Alicia Manzano and Circle Leader Miranda and daughter from Albuquerque, New Mexico

Second, Circles is different from other national programs that teach individuals that the path out of poverty is to master rules of how to speak and act like a mythic "middle-class person" or that dismiss the pervasiveness and impact of discrimination based on race, ethnicity, gender, sexual orientation, undocumented status, or lack of language proficiency. Circles is a "real world" capacity and community-building approach. We recognize that even when Circle Leaders dress professionally, speak in a formal way, develop a clear plan for financial stability, and use the resources available to them, there still may be employers, financial aid officers at community colleges, police personnel and health care providers who judge them as "just not trying hard enough to find work," or not "pulling themselves up by their bootstraps." If the Circle Leader is a person of color and a single mom, she might be stereotyped as "having babies to get more welfare." It is much more effective to talk about real world experiences and to develop realistic strategies for countering such views. Our work together must be "real" and relevant or it isn't useful.

Erica and Rose, Circles staff from Pitcairn, Pennsylvania

Third, Circles not only recognizes the value of relationships, and the benefits of cross-class relationships, but we also talk about how to develop and sustain relationships. We talk about disagreements that might emerge, since they do in all relationships; we talk about conflict and how to manage it. We have meetings that celebrate the gifts we each bring to the Circles community and show everyone their leadership potential. This means we offer information, skill building and opportunities to try out leadership skills, for instance, in a supportive community.

Fourth, both communities and individuals are required to work together to develop longer-term, sustainable strategies to move families out of poverty. Other "band-aid" programs and services are short-term fixes that don't have long-term results. When a two-year Circle Leader summed up his experience, he said it was "an uphill climb." A sustainable approach to moving folks out of poverty takes long-term investment by community members and volunteers, political advocacy, collaboration and hard work. The Big View takes a big investment of persistence. Often groups start small and then grow their efforts. The Circles Big View team in Albuquerque set their sights on increasing options for low-income housing that would be safe. They were successful in persuading the City Council not to cut the funding earmarked for a new development for low-income families. Inviting a local state senator to a Big View meeting to hear about the cliff effect and hear Circle Leaders describe how it affected their lives started important conversations and discussions about how to collaborate with Big View research efforts being pursued in other states such as Colorado.

These are just a few of the reasons I have been grateful for my work with Circles and gratified to see the potential realized again and again. My story has been made all the richer by the stories of so many who work with and are touched by Circles. Meeting Scott Miller was just the beginning; may his vision continue to expand Circles and encourage communities to thrive!

Circles from the Perspective of a Community Psychologist
By Gordon Hannah, Ph.D.

When I first heard about Circles in 2005, I had just completed a Ph.D. in community psychology. Community psychology is the branch of psychology that attempts to address social problems by applying the principles of psychology at the level of the community or organization (rather than working with individual clients). While in my program, I had researched various social problems in order to decide the direction of my future career. In community psychology (and epidemiology), there are a number of criteria used to determine where to place limited resources when addressing multiple problems: incidence (how many people are affected), severity (how debilitating the problem is to the people affected and to society), and preventability/treatability (how easy or hard would it be to prevent or treat the problem with existing resources).

In 2014, 43.6 million Americans lived in poverty, including 16.7 million children, as determined by the U.S. poverty threshold. By comparison, 1.2 million Americans are a victim of violent crime each year, 1.7 million are diagnosed with cancer, and 0.7 million suffer a heart attack. The consequences of living in poverty, especially over a prolonged period, are severe. Those living in poverty in the United States have an average life expectancy 6.5 years shorter than those who are affluent. Low income Americans are more likely to suffer from virtually every physical health problem from headaches, flu, and colds to cancer, diabetes, and heart attacks, while also having less access to health care. Individuals with family incomes below $15,000 are over three times more likely to be victims of violent crime than individuals with family incomes greater than $75,000.

Children living in poverty are at greater risk for poor academic achievement, school dropout, abuse and neglect, behavioral and socio emotional problems, and developmental delays. Living in poverty negatively affects cognitive development of preschool age and early school age children, resulting in lower cognitive abilities (six to 13 points on standardized tests of IQ). Economists estimate that child poverty costs $500 billion per year to the U.S. economy.

In many ways, however, the worst impact of poverty is to exclude millions of people from meaningful participation and contribution to our society and instead forcing them into a marginalized position of dependency. Unlike some social ills, the pathway out of poverty (at least within the United States) is well understood. Education and employment serve both as prevention and "treatment." We do not need to wait for a scientist to discover a "cure" for poverty before we can act. We can eradicate poverty now! Based on these statistics and thoughts, I decided to focus my career on ending poverty.

After I graduated, I accepted a professorship at Indiana University of Pennsylvania in Indiana, Pennsylvania. Soon after my arrival, I visited the human service organizations in town that were working to address poverty and offered my services. I was very fortunate to meet Sandi Dill, who was then Director of the Indiana County Community Action Program. She was considering starting a new program called Circles and asked me if I would be interested in helping out. As I read through the program materials, I knew that I had found what I was looking for. Circles contained many of the elements of effective interventions advocated by community psychology. Circles is empowerment oriented. It seeks to actively engage low-income people in the process of community change and places them in a position of leadership. Circles is strengths-based and focuses on what low-income people can do rather than focusing on dysfunction. Circles encourages ecological thinking about wellbeing, where well-being is not determined exclusively by an individual's characteristics nor by distant, societal forces, but rather through the interplay of an individual and the community in which they live.

One of best researched and most effective psychological interventions is motivational interviewing (or MI). MI was originally created to treat problem drinkers, but was soon expanded to help people overcome all types of addictions, weight loss, improving eating habits, increasing exercise, and behavioral change in general. MI focuses on establishing a collaborative relationship with the client rather than the typical expert-patient relationship found in traditional therapy. Rather than focusing on giving clients what they lack, MI focuses on evoking clients' own abilities, aspirations, and dreams. Perhaps most importantly, MI acknowledges clients' autonomy to choose for themselves rather than coercing them to do the "right thing." MI was born out of the realization that motivation is not a static quality of an individual, but rather a dynamic force that arises out of relationship to others. Circles shares these same effective principles: collaborative relationships, evoking aspirations, honoring autonomy, and building motivation through relationship.

The primary mechanism used in Circles to move people out of poverty is increasing their "social capital." Social capital is one's ability to access resources in a community through one's relationships with other people and institutions. Research on homelessness has found that social support and numbers of social contacts significantly predict people's ability to exit homelessness, after controlling for other factors such as alcohol use, substance use, psychiatric symptoms, and employment status. In focus groups, people who have successfully exited homelessness most frequently cite relationships with family and service providers as the factor that helped them exit homelessness. Large caseloads and services that focus on short-term stabilization, however, limit the ability of professional human service providers to provide the kind of long-term social support needed to move people permanently out of poverty. Circles' innovation of using peer support, volunteer "ally" support, and guiding coalition support to increase social capital is a major advancement over traditional services.

While in my community psychology program, I researched the effectiveness of community approaches to addressing poverty. One of the patterns I noticed was the recurrent underestimation programs made of the amount of support required by low income people to utilize effectively the services being provided. Workforce development initiatives attempt to provide training to low skill workers for entry into a particular industry. Often, these initiatives have shown disappointing results because participants lacked transportation to get to the program, lacked sufficient reading proficiency to utilize program materials, or lacked basic knowledge of workplace norms required to be successful. When you consider that most services for low income people are designed by middle- and upper-income people, it is perhaps not surprising that these barriers were overlooked. Initiatives such as comprehensive community initiatives and empowerment zones attempted to address this problem by including low-income people on administrative boards in order to give voice to such concerns.

Unfortunately, they often failed to provide sufficient leadership training and support to the low-income board members and their voices were often marginalized by those more experienced in leadership roles. Circles addresses this issue by providing everyone involved in the initiative, Circle leaders, volunteer allies, and guiding coalition members, with training on the worldviews of people from different socioeconomic and cultural groups. Circles also holds regular "big view" meetings where barriers to participation are discussed, and common barriers to participation, such as transportation and childcare, are addressed as part of the model.

The congruence between Circles and what I had learned as a community psychologist sold me. I agreed to become chair of the Indiana County Circles Guiding Coalition and watched the program go from an informal discussion among a few human service professionals to a community of churches, businesses, and volunteers working with a cohort of Circles leaders to change lives. While I found the Circles model compelling, actually working face-to-face with families and seeing a family move from desperate circumstances to being co-chair of our Circles Guiding Coalition compelled me on a much deeper level. Circles helped me learn how to work more collaboratively with people from all parts of the community, to focus more on relationships rather than just on "achieving results," and informed me on a personal level about both the toll of poverty on individual lives and the power of people to overcome adversity when provided with opportunity. I consider my time with Circles to be the most rewarding experience of my professional life. I now live in Pittsburgh, Pennsylvania and am working with Circles USA and local organizations to support multiple Circles chapters in an attempt to widen the impact of Circles at a citywide level. I am excited to see where Circles takes me next!

Zack Block, Director of Repair the World, and Akirah Robinson, Family Care Coordinator for Open Hand Ministries at a Circles Pittsburgh planning event in the offices of Repair the World

Chapter 6: A Call to Action!

I first want to thank all of the contributors to this book for their wonderful stories, and for the groundbreaking work that they are doing in their communities. They all play a timely and important role in inspiring and equipping our society with practical know-how on what people really need from the community, public policy, schools, businesses and the economy in order to escape poverty.

In order to move the needle in our communities and begin reducing poverty, all sectors of our community need to commit to high levels of research and innovation in order to achieve new results. Businesses will need to update their human resource practices in order to tap the currently unqualified talent pool in their own community. Education must align with the forecasts of the economic development field in order to prepare students for the jobs of the future. Government must eliminate public policy barriers like the cliff effects and attach programs like Circles onto their basic services so that people do not need to keep using government assistance. Philanthropy must invest longer and deeper into high-impact strategies that transform people and systems. And the community at large must get involved in building deeper connections with one another so that no family or child is abandoned to the distresses of poverty.

Is there a tipping point that we can strive to reach that would change our communities enough to eventually eradicate poverty? We believe there is and we are committed to pursuing the research to find out. What if we start by making a commitment to support at least 10% of our community's households living below 150% of the Federal Poverty Guidelines (FPG) to earn at least 200% of the FPG? What would a community have to do to accomplish this goal? It would have to transform its approach to poverty in the following ways:

1. **Consult with those living in poverty** as you engage in planning because they are your experts. If you are currently experiencing poverty, or have experienced it some time in your life, you can provide an "expert voice" that is so necessary for community

planning processes. You can bring both insights and urgency that people like me, who have been raised in middle and upper income backgrounds, often lack. Consider joining a board of directors, or a speaker's bureau. If you have Circles already in your community, you can join one of our community teams organized to sustain and expand Circles. Speak out! Your community needs your voice.

2.   **Commit to the long haul** by establishing a long-term support system, like Circles. If you have influence with funders and/or community program leaders, discuss the enormous benefits of providing people with consistent, long-term support to transform their lives and become economically secure and stable. Community programs that provide emergency assistance and short-term training or counseling services can then refer people to Circles to solve the underlying problems and achieve major goals.

3.   **Eliminate the dangerous "cliff effects"** so that people can safely transition from assistance programs into jobs. Communities would have to ask their state policy makers to remove the disincentives known as the "cliff effects" so that people can earn more income without being penalized with disproportionate drops in assistance. For example, one Circle Leader here in Albuquerque would lose her Medicaid coverage for her son when she earns $2,491 a month. When we did this analysis with her, she was earning $2,400 a month. If she earned another $100 per month, we estimated that she would need to spend several hundred per month more to cover his new health insurance, or drop his health insurance altogether. It was a lose-lose scenario. Furthermore, there was no available calculator to help her and other Circle Leaders in her group to determine the cliff effects in advance of hitting them. This is a relatively "easy fix" that must be made by federal, state, and local governmental programs in order to reduce poverty.

4.   **Design individualized plans** that give people the education, training, networking support, and skills to earn at least 200% of the FPG. For a family of four, this would be $47,700 a year. There is no "one-shoe-fits-all" program. Everyone is unique and requires an economic stability plan specific to their needs.

5.   **Invest in the safety net AND long-term solutions.** Change how funders (state agencies, United Ways, foundations, corporations, etc.) finance the system of community services so that there are incentives to move programming from short-term fixes to long-term solutions. We must offer incentives for people to innovate, take risks, and learn how to do the work that really makes a difference.

6.   **Teach people about money.** If we teach our citizenry the ropes of how to make and manage money – beginning at an early age and reinforcing it each and every year until high school graduation – then we will be giving the next generation the necessary tools to be successful within our economic system. To thrive in North America, or practically anywhere else in the world, one must learn how to earn, manage, and invest money. We have not systematically taught financial literacy in our schools and we are now paying dearly for that mistake.

For example, according to the AARP, nearly half of older Americans rely on Social Security payments, (which average $1,200 a month), as their principle source of income. The median retirement account balance for all working-age households in the United States amounts to a total of only $3,000. More than 50% of these households don't have a retirement savings plan of any kind. We have a financially illiterate society, which is vulnerable to relying on predatory lenders to make ends meet during desperate times. The FDIC broadly defines predatory lending as "making unfair and abusive loan terms on borrowers." Only 15 states currently ban predatory lending. In the other 35 states, predatory lenders are free to target the elderly, low-income families, and others, like those escaping domestic violence, with lending programs that charge exorbitant interest rates in exchange for emergency funds. In 2012, approximately $29.8 billion in loans were made at payday stores, and another $14.3 billion online. We can change this going forward by making a commitment to teaching financial literacy and banning predatory lending in all 50 states.

Circle from Albuquerque, New Mexico

The Call to Action!

I urge you to look at your own *circle of influence* and bring your personal leadership to the task of changing programs, policies, and people's hearts and minds so that we can end poverty sooner than later. Here is an initial list of what you can do to improve the lives of others and contribute to your community's economic wellbeing:

1.   **EDUCATE YOURSELF** and your **ELECTED OFFICIALS** about barriers to getting out of poverty, like the predatory lending practices in your state and community. If there are little to no protections for those in poverty, then educate your elected officials and ask them to address the problem.

     Learn more about the cliff effects for your state. Look on the Internet or call your local government programs to understand that, if your family was living below the federal poverty guidelines, at what level of new earned income would you lose cash assistance, food stamps, childcare assistance, housing assistance, and/or health insurance. If you cannot determine this through your own research, imagine what it is like for someone who may not have access to a computer, or who is caught in the middle of day-to-day financial crises. Again, educate your elected officials and ask that these programs provide easy-to-use calculators, and more importantly, that they eliminate the cliff effects so that people can earn more income and be better off, not worse off for it.

2.   **GET INVOLVED** in your local economic development strategies. Resolving poverty will require that the community has enough well-paying jobs to offer its employable workforce. The economic development strategies of the 20th century are most likely not going to be effective for the 21th century economy. Businesses may have to look toward tapping currently "unqualified" candidates in their community to fill jobs, requiring a different commitment to "qualifying" people for the workforce. Solving poverty is both a humanitarian and an economic development strategy. To help your community to attract and/or grow new jobs, get involved in the economic development plans for your community and advocate for moving people off assistance programs and into the qualified job market.

3.   **TALK MONEY** to your school board and administration and ask that they formally teach financial literacy to all children. Offer to mentor children in how to manage money. Support children in learning how to make money as entrepreneurs. There are endless opportunities for children to be involved in community fundraising events, which will teach them invaluable lessons in making money, as well as the value of providing community service.

4.   **INVEST in HIGH-IMPACT PROGRAMS**. Call people who work at your local United Way, community foundations, community service programs and/or government agencies and ask them what agency currently receives funding to help people earn at least 200% of the federal poverty guidelines. Does anyone have long-term (more than a year) results to

show you? If you find such a program, ask how you can help them to support more people out of poverty. If no such program exists, then consider educating funders and community service directors about Circles and what it would take to bring it to town.

5.   **GIVE YOUR TIME, TALENT and TREASURE** to those who are suffering from poverty. If you already have Circles in your community, or once it begins, there are many opportunities to support people out of poverty and address the systemic problems that contribute to conditions that exacerbate poverty. While many volunteers choose to be Allies, hundreds of others choose to help in other ways, like organizing weekly meals, providing childcare assistance, tutoring children, driving people to job interviews, helping people write resumes, providing budgeting support, etc. There are also countless ways that people can get involved in addressing the systemic problems, such as writing letters to policy makers, speaking to community groups, writing blogs, etc.

When we enter into relationships with people who have been suffering with poverty, we see how daunting the challenges are that these families face on a daily basis. People in poverty have often experienced physical and emotional trauma that undermines their ability to achieve their long-term goals. They have little to no money to invest in education in order to get ahead. Many have health problems that they do not have enough money to pay for treatments, or in many cases, the gas money to get themselves to treatments. Their cars are old and unreliable, or they must use the public transportation system, which in most areas of the country is limited. We have not taught financial education in our schools, so many people have simply learned the ropes from the previous generation, which in many cases was also living in poverty. Yes, people must take personal responsibility, and yes, we must change our systems. It is not one or the other as our media and politics would have us believe. Ending poverty means simultaneously supporting both systemic change and personal responsibility.

People need long-term support to permanently transform their economic and social conditions. Circles is designed to bring the best that public programs have to offer people with the best informal supports available through community-minded Allies. Circles gives people the opportunities that they really need to stabilize their lives and eventually thrive. We also provide Circle Leaders with the opportunity to reach back and become an Ally to the next person, completing their own circle.

What it would be like to live in a world that is free of the conditions of poverty? We have normalized poverty for so long that it might be hard for any of us to even imagine such a future. I am certain, however, that we will all sleep better at night knowing that every child is being fed and provided for, and that they are being effectively prepared for the real world of earning and managing money, and contributing to the economic vitality of their communities. As a society, we know enough now to become serious about ending poverty. You can personally help to bring this important vision to reality by doing whatever you think will make the most difference in your community.

As Rebecca told us in her story, "America, you need me to tell you there is hope for the direction our nation is going. You need to hear that there is still an American dream and that families on the lowest rung of the economic ladder can still lasso that dream. A couple of years ago, I would have grimaced at a conversation like that. Today with tears in my eyes, I can tell you I am living proof."

May you go forth and help others to prosper!

-Scott C. Miller

Chapter 7: Steps to Starting Circles

1. **Contact Circles USA**
    www.circlesusa.org
    888-232-9285
    Gena@circlesusa.org
    We will send you the Circles Assessment Tool

2. **Convene**
    Convene your local partners to explore Circles and to go through the Assessment Tool together to determine if Circles is right for your community at this time.

3. **Plan**
    If you decide you want to bring Circles to your community, Circles USA will help you develop a solid foundation through its planning process.

4. **Train**
    Once you determine who is going to do what through the planning process, Circles USA will provide you with training so that everyone knows what their job is and how to do it.

5. **Begin**
    Once all the roles and responsibilities have been assigned and people have been trained, you can begin enrolling people into the Circles process. Circles USA will provide you with tools, coaching, and other supports to help you succeed with Circles!

Visit us at:
www.CirclesUSA.org
www.twitter.com/CirclesUSA
www.facebook.com/circlesusa
https://www.linkedin.com/company/move-the-mountain-leadership-center

Notes

Made in the USA
Middletown, DE
25 August 2016